This book marks the first ti... "pristine," Yi King has ever bee... the *true* order of the Hexagrams ...Kly memorize their order and thei... ...g. You will also learn how the playing of chess can easily be incorporated with Yi King divination.

In this book you will discover the history of the Yi King. It has gone through five evolutions and much has been added to its original simplicity. You will also discover how the Yi King was originally used and how you can easily use it today without referring to any books.

Louis Culling, renowned occultist and expert on the Yi King, undertook the task of "scraping away the barnacles," as he put it, that had fastened themselves onto the Yi over the centuries. In fact, much of the material in the most popular edition of the I Ching was added and not part of the original work. Most of that book is based on an invention of about the 11th century. Fu Hsi had given forth the foundation of the Yi King 4,000 years prior to this recent invention.

The additions were created by King Wan. While imprisoned he used the time to compose the text of the Hexagrams. He wrote from the viewpoint of a "Great One," advising rules for a good government and comparing it to the inefficiency of the presiding ruler. There was much instruction as to how his followers could and should carry out the military campaign against the evil ruler and his low cohorts. For this reason, King Wan deliberately obscured much of the true meaning of the text as a way to protect himself from further inciting the government. He also put the Hexagrams in such an illogical and incongruous order that it was obviously a secret code.

If you want to learn the secrets of the real, *pristine* Yi King, then you should read this book. *The Pristine Yi King* promises to revolutionize the way people think about this classic book of wisdom forever!

About the Author

Louis T. Culling, who died in 1973, was a man whose mind had a tremendous reach and vitality, whose life had been one of adventure and fulfillment, and whose contributions to modern occultism are unique.

In the early 1930s, Mr. Culling joined the magical Order G∴B∴G∴, which was founded in the United States by C. F. Russell and fashioned after Aleister Crowley's A∴A∴. He acted for some time as the head of the Southern California section of the Order.

Mr. Culling was also an expert on the Yi King, which he called the *Pristine Yi King* to differentiate it from the orthodox I Ching, which espouses Chinese philosophy but ignores what he felt to be the intent of the original Yi. *The Pristine Yi King* represents 30 years' research by Mr. Culling in the Yi King.

To Write to the Publisher

The publisher does appreciate hearing from readers, learning of your enjoyment and benefit from this book. Llewellyn also publishes a bi-monthly news magazine with news and reviews of practical esoteric studies and articles helpful to the student, and some readers' questions and comments to the author may be answered through this magazine's columns if permission to do so is included in the original letter. To ask a question, write to the editor of *The Llewellyn New Times*:

Editor
The Llewellyn New Times
P.O. Box 64383-107, St. Paul, MN 55164-0383, U.S.A.

About Llewellyn's Inner Guide Series

Each of us faces in two directions, like the alchemists' double-headed Phoenix risen from ashes and born again.

In one direction, we face the Outer World—and know that should we ignore this world we suffer and die; in the other direction we face the Inner World—which all too commonly we ignore to our peril!

It is to this Inner World we now turn—without ignoring the Outer one—to avoid the perils facing all humankind. To meet the challenges of today, we need new Awareness, and new sources of Knowledge and Power—and these may be found only within the Ultimate Source from which all have their being, and that way lies within.

The Western Esoteric Tradition—in its Mystery Schools, Magical Orders, and Secret Lodges—has taught many techniques for Inner Awareness and growth to those who have sought out such wisdom. Their guidance has been there, accessible to the few who could be provided for by the Lodge system, filling the needs of the times.

Now the time has come to expand access to these esoteric techniques beyond the limitations of the Lodge, and to publish them in modern form for the benefit of the many. *Just as humankind stands at the edge of Outer Space, so must we—simultaneously—explore the Paths and Worlds of Inner Space.*

Each book in the Inner Guide series, as in Llewellyn's Practical Guide series, is self-contained and complete in presentation—yet each is also like a building-block that can be placed anywhere in the personal structure that is your evolving self. Practical Guides build your inner talents for application in the outer world; Inner Guides direct your inward growth—yet, they too, have measurable effect in the outer world, for both benefit the Whole Person.

Carl Llewellyn Weschcke

Other books by Louis Culling:

Sex Magick

The Complete Magick Curriculum of the Secret Order G∴B∴G∴

The Incredible I Ching

The L.R.I. I Ching

Llewellyn's Inner Guide Series

The Pristine Yi King

The Pure Wisdom of Ancient China

by Louis T. Culling

1989
Llewellyn Publications
St. Paul, Minnesota, 55164-0383, U.S.A.

International Standard Book Number: 0-87542-107-5

First Edition, 1989
First Printing, 1989

**Cover Painting: Susan McDonnell
Diagrams: Christopher Wells**

Produced by Llewellyn Publications
Typography and Art property of Chester-Kent, Inc.

Published by
**LLEWELLYN PUBLICATIONS
A Division of Chester-Kent, Inc.**
P.O. Box 64383
St. Paul, MN 55164-0383, U.S.A.

Printed in the United States of America

Table of Contents

Foreword

I have known of the Yi King for several decades. It was late in 1928 that I watched Aleister Crowley operate the sticks, in his apartment in Paris, to obtain some augury for the ensuing period. He had also written a poetic interpretation of the Yi King hexagrams which I studied there in Paris. In *Liber 777* he provided a long string of mythological attributions to these figures.

However, I cannot truthfully say that any of this material meant very much to me. The Qabalah and characteristically Western types of divination, philosophy, and mysticism seemed more sympathetic to my understanding, while the Yi was essentially foreign and obscure.

The result was that I mostly left the system alone. Occasionally I would make sporadic attempts to read about it—Jung's essay on the Yi, for example, written as an introduction to Wilhelm's German translation of the ancient Chinese classic—but nothing there really gripped me in such a way as to motivate me to study the system.

Thus things stood for many years. In 1964, during a casual conversation with Louis Culling, I suggested he write a couple of articles about the Yi for the English periodical *New Dimensions*. The outcome was the delightful little book entitled *The Incredible I Ching*, published in 1965 by Helios Publishing Company in England. More than anything else I know, this is a little masterpiece, despite the smallness of its size, which naturally limits the extent of clarification and elucidation. It opened many doors for me. I am sure it has done so for others, too.

The current text, *The Pristine Yi King,* continues along the same lines, but carries the subject further and explains a great deal more.

Make no mistake about it, the book is good. It is a fine exposition of basic principles, demonstrating some profound insights. The book therefore can be honestly recommended for serious study. The average student who has never before made any sense out of this ancient system can be assured that here, for the first time, some clear light will be shed. It will enable him or her to approach the original texts with confidence and assurance and also to attempt divination, if so s/he will, with more than a superficial understanding of what s/he is doing. This I believe is the clearest indication that the author has succeeded in his original intention.

ISRAEL REGARDIE
Studio City, California
January 27, 1966

Preface

It was on a Sunday evening in the spring of 1938 that I met Louis Culling at the Gnostic Mass of the O.T.O. in Hollywood, California (see *Magick in Theory and Practice* by Aleister Crowley). This dramatic ritual was most impressively done with dignity and beauty—it was a source of great inspiration, both to the participating members as well as to the audience.

From that moment we felt a kinship that lasted for 35 years—until the time of his death in 1973. Over these years we spent much time in study, discussion, and writing. Mr. Culling was a maverick—a rugged individualist—ever delving into obscure subjects and expounding upon them. It was not until a few years before his death that he became recognized as the knowledgeable person he really was.

We spent many hours over a cup of tea, trying to solve all the riddles of the universe! His knowledge of music was extensive (he was a theater organist by profession for many years), so we also found a mutual interest on that level. It seems all occult work is in some way allied to the arts, and many of us who are interested in or participate in the arts also gravitate to the occult. Perhaps it is the dramatic quality of both fields that intrigues us so.

At the time of our meeting in 1938, Mr. Culling was acting Neighborhood Primate of the San Diego

Lodge of the G∴B∴G∴. This was a Gnostic Order founded by a disciple of Aleister Crowley, and it is now defunct—unfortunately. I was just a beginner at that time, so Mr. Culling served as a source of much inspiration and guidance through the period when I was so arduously trying to assimilate the teachings and pass the various Grades in it.

The study and application of the principles of the Yi King were an essential part of the G∴B∴G∴ Order. It was during this time that Mr. Culling started his research on the subject, gathering information from many sources, over and above what was required by the Order. It was in those early days that the germ of this present book had its inception, and I have considered it a great privilege to have helped prepare this copy for publication.

However, at the time Mr. Culling was gathering these notes together to present it in the present book form, he was already a very ill man with emphysema, and much of the pertinent material was overlooked. Without changing the text and Mr. Culling's own particular style of writing, I have endeavored to work around some of these discrepancies.

The Yi King is a most profound and intriguing system of philosophy and divination. It is based on the polarity of opposites. It is quite evident that we virtually live and move in a vast sea of energy that is subject to the arrangements, patterns, and polarities of these ever constant, yet ever changing, forces. All manifestation is subject to this Law, which on this plane manifests as Duality. Everything is in the process of seeking its equilibrium, and it is in this working of the energies that change is constantly taking place. Aleister Crowley once said: "The stability of the universe is change." The Yang is the positive principle and the Yin the negative. Yang is electric in quality; Yin is magnetic. All manifestation on this earth is evolved from this interplay and union of these two principles and the many variations of it, as expressed in the 64 Hexagrams of the Logical Square.

The magickal figure of 64 is evident in the 64 logical equations by which an idea may be expressed. Chess is a game of logic. The cube, with its eight sides, also contains the number 64, and the cube unfolded becomes the Cross of Matter upon which the whole "game" of Life is being played.

In music there are 64 measures that complete an idea. The first four measures are the germ of the melody—the subject. The next four measures must indeed follow to provide the predicate. In eight measures the complete theme is manifest. Sixteen measures unfold this theme, then 32 extend it or expand it, until 64 have been arrived at and the complete musical idea is fully informed. The rest of the composition is merely a repetition or further embellishment upon what was started in the first eight measures.

One question Mr. Culling and I could never quite resolve: Are the figures we cast the result of our own subconscious mind, or is it the result of the intervention of superconscious Intelligences? Mr. Culling thought it safer to "follow the *due mien*," and arbitrated by saying it was the "supraconscious" mind of the operator. In the G∴B∴G∴ Order we were most definitely told it was the result of superconscious Intelligences using the Yi King as an instrument to communicate the higher Wisdom to man.

No matter which is correct, we both agreed that proper preparation in the form of a brief ritual or prayer was effective in obtaining the best result of the question. The question should be sincere and simply put, allowing a general scope for the answer. In other words, ask a silly question and you will get a silly answer! But anyone who will take the time and patience to study the Yi King with sincerity is not apt to ask a silly question in the first place!

The essential requirement to obtain a correct and responsive figure is dedication and a proper attitude of mind. The more we can lift our consciousness to the level of higher thinking and feeling, the better and easier it is to make contact with higher Intelligences or even with our own "supraconscious" mind. Crowley said: "Enflame thyself with prayer!"

Whatever method is used to cast a Hexagram—be it dice, wands, or even coins—the whole operation should be performed with *absolute sincerity of mind and purpose*. And the more one works with this system, the more one gradually grows into a more dedicated attitude toward the Yi King.

I have used all the methods explained in this book, but I find that the coin method is the easiest and the most simple. If one person is casting, the figure should be built from the lower line up. If two persons are casting, usually a man and a woman, the woman makes the first throw and builds the lower Trigram. The man throws and builds the upper Trigram. Each takes turns with the coin until it has been cast three times by each one. I have used this method for many years and it always worked very well.

In the G∴B∴G∴ Order we were required to make the Logical Square from memory. This is not as difficult as it may seem when one has properly organized his or her thinking with the basic structures of the Trigrams (see Table 1 in this text). This Logical Square was drawn on a piece of white cloth about 24 x 24 inches, and the casting was made on this. The fact that we had to make it from memory was a magickal gesture in itself, and this imbued it with one's own magickal force. Each casting was preceded with a brief ritual or prayer to elevate the conscious mind to its attunement with, as Mr. Culling describes it, the supraconscious.

It is interesting to note that in plate II, figure 1 of the Legge translation of the I Ching, the diagram of Fu-Hsi (see Table 2 of *The Pristine Yi King*) closely approximates the arrangement of the Logical Order. However, it is *reversed*. By turning the page around, the entire arrangement falls into its proper logical order. In plate III, figure 2, the comparison is made between that of King Wan and Fu-Hsi, which substantiates the above. Mr. Culling explains in *The Pristine Yi King* that King Wan deliberately arranged the figures in this manner for political reasons: to make them so obscure that only one who had the key could make any sense out of it.

For many years scholars have referred to the Legge and Wilhelm translations as if they were the only standard books on the subject. Fortunately, now we have this work of Louis Culling, *The Pristine Yi King—*

the Logical Order—to guide us through this intricate and extensive system of philosophy and divination. This is an achievement no other scholar has ever attempted. It is with great pride and joy that this book is presented to the searching public.

THAYNNE W. PATTERSON

(5°=□—G∴B∴G∴)
North Hollywood, Calif.
April 7, 1976

1 The Yi King

The title of this book was chosen as the result of my having outlined and fully treated the essence and purity of the original *Pa Kua* (Trigrams) of Fu Hsi. I have endeavored to delete all extraneous accretions, which are like barnacles grown and multiplied throughout the centuries. All these barnacles must be scraped away before the now heavily encrusted Yi King can be seen in all its purity.

To my knowledge, this is the first time that the *pure* Yi King has been given in print. In saying this, I do not supernumerate the mantle of Elijah and intimate that the gods have appointed me as the chosen one! There are plenty of keys for discovering the original Yi King. They are contained in the original Pa Kua, and there is much in the writings of King Wan and his son in discerning the wheat from the chaff.

It is assumed that most people who are interested in the Yi know about the two major translations of the texts. One is *The I Ching or Book of Changes*, translated by Wilhelm and Baynes, and the other is *I Ching Book of Changes*, translated by Legge. Legge is a recognized sinologist, and although Wilhelm was not an academic sinologist, he had recourse to the help of two Chinese men who were, so we are told, Masters of the Yi.

Previous to these two works there had been a translation in Latin by P. Regis and another one in English by the Reverend Canon McClatchie in 1876. McClatchie's book is not easily obtainable. I have not seen it, but I am inclined to recommend it because of Legge's comment that the Reverend had applied the key of comparative mythology (and phallicism) and had "found sundry things not too pleasant to look or dwell upon." However, there is no correspondence between the Yi King and the inhibitions of Legge and Wilhelm on the subject of Yang and Yin.

It is not my intention to make a series of attacks upon other writers of the Yi, despite the fact that I was deeply shocked to see the mass of material in the Wilhelm-Baynes book that most definitely has no part in the original pure text of the Yi. Much of their work is based on an invention of about the 11th century of our present era, and Fu-Hsi had given forth the foundation of the Yi King 4,000 years prior to this invention! The shock of this instigated the writing of this book.

A History of the Yi King

By tradition, the eight Pa Kua of the Yi King, now called Trigrams, were originally given forth by Fu-Hsi in 3322 B.C.. There is some question as to whether the name was actually Fu-Hsi and also some question about the date. Let us then say that Fu-Hsi is a convenient name. In regard to the date, we do know that the Trigrams had been doubled to make various Hexagrams as early as 2205 B.C.. This was after the first exposition of the eight Trigrams. Therefore it is safe to say that the original Pa Kua were first diagrammed as early as 2500 B.C.. This is only 800 years after the traditional date, so there is little cause for quibbling sophistries.

Here are the original Pa Kua of Fu-Hsi:

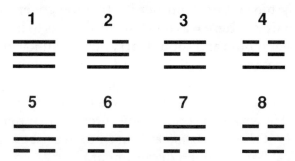

There were no names given to the eight Trigrams, nor was there one single word of explanation. Later in this book it will be shown why explanations were not necessary.

The doubling of the Trigrams, one above the other to form the Hexagrams, constitutes the *second evolution* (circa 2205 B.C.) of the eight Pa Kua. This process stems from something basic in the human mind and psychology.

The *third evolution* was by King Wan, circa 1150 B.C. By all available records he was the first man to give names of meaning to the 64 Hexagrams (resulting from the doubling of the eight Trigrams in all possible combinations). He also gave a very brief explanation about the name of each Hexagram and whether or not it was advantageous for progress.

King Wan composed these texts while imprisoned for political reasons. He wrote from the viewpoint of a "Great One," advising rules for a good government and comparing it to the inefficiency of the presiding ruler. It was for this reason that King Wan deliberately obscured much of the order of the texts as a way of protecting himself from further inciting the government of that time. There was much instruction as to how his followers could and should carry out the military campaign against the evil ruler and his low cohorts. For this reason he put the Hexagrams in such an illogical and incongruous order that it was obviously a secret code. He wrote, to some extent, after the manner of a diviner. (The word *diviner* is used to describe one of high caliber and deep discernment.)

The *fourth evolution* came two years after the work of King Wan. His son, Due of Kau, wrote what he considered to be the implications of each of the six lines of the 64 Hexagrams.

The *fifth evolution* consists of the seven appendices contained in Legge's translation. They are included here because Kung Fu-tse (Confucious) is said to have had some words in it. Contained in this collection are bushels of chaff in which are a few quarts of wheat. There are some comments contained that give support to my thesis.

Accretions and mutations in the evolution. The one and only account *in print* of ancient origin is presented here solely as evidence of the unauthentic system given in the Wilhelm-Baynes book.

The ancient tradition states that a tortoise or sea-horse came up out of the Ho River. The markings on its back gave Fu-Hsi the idea for his Trigrams. These markings on the back of the creature were black and white. The black was attributed to Yin and the white to Yang. This Ho River "map" is mentioned in the Shu records as having been preserved at Court in 1079 B.C. Beyond this date it was lost for all time. There was only a speculative reproduction of the Ho Map given to the public during the reign of Hui Zung of the Sung Dynasty of A.D. 1101–1125. This was an invention of the 12th century A.D.

The odd numbers were considered as Yang and the even numbers as Yin. The markings arranged themselves thus:

$$4 \quad 9 \quad 2$$
$$3 \quad 5 \quad 7$$
$$8 \quad 1 \quad 6$$

This is nothing but an arithmetical puzzle in which the numbers from one to nine add to 15, in whatever way we add them. These numbers can also be arranged in other ways to obtain the same results.

Therefore we have no reason to believe that in A.D.

1101 the lost Ho Map of 1079 B.C. was correctly guessed. Even if the modern Ho River Map is the same as the original, it has no place in the original Yi as a method of erecting the Hexagram; nor is there any efficacy in the method of interpretation as expounded in the Wilhelm-Baynes work.

These five evolutions and the mutations will be explained in the succeeding chapters. From the analysis of them will be distilled the pure, original Yi King. There are methods of checking and double-checking that can be applied in all of the foregoing historical evolutions.

One may wonder about the sudden growing interest in the Yi King among Western peoples. What sparked this interest of the past 30 years? There is no mystery about it. C.G. Jung played the part of a James Legge in this drama.

Jung had become the favored psychologist among occult students due to his foreword and afterword in Richard Wilhelm's book *The Secret of the Golden Flower.* In his memoirs Jung writes: "Wilhelm had been the perfect disciple of the Chinese sage, Lau Nai Suan, the fulfillment of the wish dream of the sage. Wilhelm seemed completely Chinese in outward manner as much as in his way of writing and speaking. The point of view of ancient Chinese culture had penetrated him through and through."

Jung was certainly astute enough to see that Wilhelm had been the ideal medium between the old East and the modern West—the medium of transmission rather than of any unique wisdom of Wilhelm the man. Jung had been intensely interested in the psychology of primitive peoples and ancient cultures. Here was the very root of his "mass collective unconscious": He seized upon Wilhelm as the *Magickal Link* with old China.

One injects or endows one's Magickal Link with all sorts of magickal powers. Consequently he lauded Wilhelm quite beyond the realm of dispassionate evaluation. One actually wonders if Jung had aided and abetted Wilhelm's "Numinesum" and his increased *persona* (mask), which in Wilhelm's later years, upon his return from the West, prompted Jung's observation and account as follows:

In Wilhelm the European element was gaining priority over the Orient again. In such a process, without a strong conscious attempt to come to terms with it, the unconscious conflict can seriously affect the physical state of health. I attempted to call his attention to the danger threatening him.

Wilhelm replied: "I think you are right. Something here is overpowering me, but what can be done?" If Wilhelm's method and understanding of the I Ching (the German spelling for Yi King) was as great as vaunted, why did he not cast a Hexagram to determine what could be done?

The foregoing history is an attempt to explain how and why Jung had written such fantastic praise of Wilhelm's *I Ching*—which, incidentally, thereby assured no small sale for the book.

Actually, in one part of his mind, he was dubious

about writing such glowing praise. He even put the question to the Yi and came up with the Hexagram of Moon of Moon. Jung admits that this is one of the most unfavorable of the Hexagrams, but he let Wilhelm talk him out of taking the meaning of the figure in a literal manner. Wilhelm took recourse to that strange, devious manner, or rationalization, that is so dear to the hearts of the fortunetellers, many followers of the occult, and no small number of psychologists. Indeed, the method highly intrigued Jung, and that was his reason for favoring Wilhelm's book rather than that of Legge.

After Jung had cast three Hexagrams about various questions on the book and had interpreted them, he admits: "Any number of answers would have been possible. Any person of clever and versatile mind can turn the whole thing around and show how I projected my subjective contents into the symbolism of the Hexagrams."

I do not object to any of this—in fact I condone it. Certainly one must have the gift of intuition, ESP, psyche, etc. in all matters of divination. This leads us to another point: With the Pristine Yi there is a minimum amount of the psyche that is a definite requirement. On the other hand, by Wilhelm's method there is a great amount of this gift that is required.

As evidence of my detached attitude on the subject, let the following be stated: If a person favors the psychic gift method over the method of this book—which requires the memorizing of rules and their application plus the exercise of logic and synthesis—then my sincere advice is to sell this book and buy

Wilhelm's book.

This book is not an attempt to either explain or criticize the texts of King Wan and his son, nor does it supplement the works of Legge and Wilhelm. This is an exposition of the original Pristine Yi, and as such bears small relation with the foregoing.

Wilhelm's work is undoubtedly a masterpiece in presenting the Chinese philosophy and the development of Chinese divination, of which all have employed a later developed Yi King as a type of background. Regardless of the greatness of his work, it contains very little of the original Yi. I repeat: It is a great work on both Chinese philosophy and on the later-developed Yi King, which is essentially based on the Chinese philosophy.

The original Yi is based upon the eight Pa Kua and their doubling. There were no words. Therefore, although given forth by the Chinese sage Fu-Hsi, the original Yi is not even Chinese, but just high initiated wisdom, *per se.*

Essentially, the Pristine Yi King is a cosmology—a diagram of the microcosm (man) in relation to the macrocosm (the world at large). The first basic concept of this cosmology is that *all manifestation* depends upon two great cosmic principles: YANG and YIN. Yang is the male principle in all nature; Yin is its complement, the female principle. Yang and Yin are never to be regarded as constituting an antagonistic dualism; rather, they are two great *coequal, cooperating partners.* Yang by itself and Yin by itself are only abstractions until they unite, or cooperate.

All that King Wan did for the Yi was to give the 64 doubled Trigrams names—a name for each Hexagram. There is only one value obtainable from King Wan's work: He gave good, meaningful names to over half of the Hexagrams, and this proves that he knew the original Yi fairly well. Wan's son, in giving the supposed meanings of the six lines of each Hexagram, deviated from the original Yi. He treated the six lines as six parts of an integral Hexagram; and there is no such thing in the Yi as a Hexagram. Rather, it is considered as being two Trigrams—one of which is the "superior" and the other the "inferior." We have corroborating testimony of this from many sources—from the classical appendices of Legge and those of Wilhelm, who quotes in Volume I, page 383:

As previously has been pointed out, the "hexagram" should not be thought of as merely made up of six individual lines, but *always* as composed of two primary trigrams.

With this in mind, the reader will readily see that this book essays no explanations of other texts and books. It is confined to the original Pristine Yi. Because of this alone, it is the clearest, most concise and most logical of all that has been written on the Yi.

2 Divination

I n this book I will be using the words *divination* and *fortunetelling* to describe two distinctly different things. Divination is of a higher order than mere fortunetelling.

One should have a grasp of the sublime cosmology and philosophy of the Pristine Yi before attempting divination—and most certainly of the methods and rules of divination as revealed in this book.

We shall begin with the simplest methods of divination—the tea leaves and the crystal ball. For these there are no rules or printed words upon which to lean. There is no cosmology for one to arrive at correspondences. The one requirement is that one have a gift of intuition, psychic sight, ESP, or whatever you will. Without this gift there is nothing. The leaves or the crystal ball only serve as a necessary *focus* for the operator's gift to operate. At best, the operator may not always feel "the spirit of the thing," and there is nothing to rely upon, such as a system with rules and focal guidance.

In simple numerology there are rules and printed descriptions of the numbers, but the cosmo-concept, if it exists, is inadequate to aid one in a really logical analysis. Numerology does not require a gift so much as in our first example, but the requirement is great enough that it does not attract wide and intelligent interest.

Astrology is another example of this. If one venerates the words of eminent men, consider the words of Prof. C. G. Jung. In his foreword to Wilhelm's *Secret of the Golden Flower,* he states that whether one entertained the idea of the validity of astrology or not, it is nevertheless the best and most complete history of the human psyche that is extant. As for the cosmology of astrology, my friend Marc Edmund Jones devoted his entire adult life to this. We once discussed the relationship of cosmology to divination at considerable length. We agreed that the better and more suitable cosmology, the better the system of divination, if it is coherent to the operator.

The greatest difficulty in astrology is its bewildering complexities. For instance, which signs of the zodiac occupy which houses, which planets occupy both signs and houses, the aspects between planets, etc. Therefore, twelve signs, ten planets, twelve houses, and four major aspects when multiplied together result in 5,760 different possible combinations. There are still others to be added to this! There are many contradictions and extenuations in delineating a horoscope.

There is no computer that could *exactly* weigh all the factors in a horoscope and then put them through a process of synthesis and make concise decisions. Astrology is not an exact science—it is an art—and one must have a gift for this art. It involves much more than intuition, though some ungifted astrologers can provide an analysis in conformity with what is lacking.

The rules of astrology for casting the horoscope designed to answer a question are most excellent. This method is known as *horary astrology*. When a question is asked, the horoscope of the exact time the question was asked contains both the question and the answer. This is another way of saying that the nature of the astro-cosmos contains also the nature of the question and the answer at that moment. However, delineating the horary chart is much more tricky than judging the natal chart.

It takes years to master all the concepts and rules of astrology, and even after so doing, it is necessary to have a certain sensitivity—a psychic gift of feeling—to consistently come up with good decisions in this art of divination. The question is most certain to arise: Is there not some good method of divination that is not so difficult to learn? Is there not some method that does not require so much intuition to derive an answer?

We answer Yes! The Pristine Yi King.

There are a few categories and rules to memorize. It is not possible to forget what one has *memorized*, and I stress this strongly. The reason for this will be explained in a later chapter under the heading Determining the

Hexagram. The same principles used in casting a horary chart will be employed for casting the *correct* applicable Hexagram. There are several methods, three of which have never appeared in print.

In referring to a correct Hexagram, I mean that it will not be a Hexagram that has been derived through blind chance, such as the two methods given in Wilhelm's work.

Wilhelm's method derives from the 11th or 12th century A.D., and was invented by fortunetellers. Since the Hexagram of any particular question was derived through a method of blind and haphazard chance, there had to be some newly invented method of interpretation. This was accomplished by introducing a complicated system of numerology as an aid in judging the figure.

As a general result, the only people who can work such a system are fortunetellers. By this system one can read or construct the answer no matter what Hexagram has been erected. It requires this very special talent typical of the ubiquitous fortuneteller, and this is a most excellent method for such minds and such proclivities. In summation: (1) There is a required, very special talent for interpretation, and (2) It has *no part* in the original Yi King. Yet no great talent or intuition is required in the pure Yi system that is revealed and explained in this book. It requires only a good deductive reasoning plus a small amount of memorized material.

All this elevates the Yi King to a position that is completely unique. I know of no other method of divination that does not require what we might, for convenience, call psychic gift.

It is my personal assumption that divination is in vain unless the subject has been initiated into *the world of Mind*. One's real identity—the real director, the Daemon, the Holy Guardian Angel, or whatever name is given to the Nameless—very often initiates the issue even though the outcome depends upon the responsive action of the subject. This responsive action—the typical "answer" of a Hexagram—indicates what one *can* do, *should* do, and should *not* do to bring about "progress and success."

In reference to the Daemon, Prof. Jung states in his *Memories, Dreams and Reflections* that there had been many instances in his life when the Daemon had practically forced him into certain attitudes, actions and projects, despite his intention of proceeding in other directions.

In many instances it has been indicated that potentiality is also involved in a good system of divination. For instance, if the question is asked: "Will I succeed as a singer?" It may well be that no one—including the querent—knows that the person cannot carry a tune, but somehow the oracle "knows," and in some form, the answer will be in the negative.

In the foreword to Wilhelm's *I Ching*, Jung has attempted to explain the *modus operandi* working behind divination. However, when his words are simplified, the summation refers to "unknown quantities involved with unknown Intelligences."

Mastery of Divination

In reading tea leaves the sole requirement is that one have the psychic gift. There are no rules. There is no involved cosmology. Astrology and the Tarot were originally fine concepts of cosmology and the relation to man. There were excellent systems of divination evolved from them, but these two systems have complex concepts and rules, and these rules must be mastered.

The Yi King was also first given forth as a cosmology—a grand cosmology, free from dogmatic concepts; yet even in this, the application of rules is essential for divination. A few basic rules are given in the following part of this book (see Appendix). They are rules so basic that one recognizes their validity and finds it easy to memorize them. However, in interpreting the meanings of the various Hexagrams there are yet other rules of a different kind.

To eliminate the necessity of mastering these rules, the nature of each of the 64 Hexagrams are extensively explained in chapter 5. The requirement of each and every Hexagram is its having an answer for hundreds of different questions. It would require a huge encyclopedia to give the application of each Hexagram to all possible questions. Therefore, we must devise a shortcut to this problem. This consists in becoming thoroughly acquainted with each figure and recognizing the uniqueness of each Hexagram. Each one is different, each unique. Then reason out the meaning of each figure from the positions and components of the upper and lower Trigrams constituting the Hexagram.

SUGGESTIONS FOR THE BEGINNER:

1. Carefully read the Hexagrams for the purpose of deriving a clear understanding of each unique figure.

2. Study the 64 Hexagrams a second time, paying particular attention to the reasoning involved in combining the nature of the two component Trigrams. This will enable you to arrive at a more clear understanding of the nature of the Hexagram.

3. Each morning, cast a figure, the question being, What will be the nature of the day both in my relations with people and with things? Do not read the meaning of the figure until the daily activities have ceased. Then, upon reading it, look for the correspondences between the nature of the Hexagram in relation to the nature of the day. Continuing this practice will bring greater clarity and understanding.

The essence of this method is to provide a coherent understanding of each of the eight Trigrams and the special significance of their position—i.e., in the upper or lower Trigram position.

In the analysis of the 64 Hexagrams it is interesting to observe that most of them are devoted to descriptions of people or their attitudes and abilities concerning the project in question. They are referred to as *inferiors* and *superiors*. There is a reason for this.

One or more persons are usually involved in various projects. In knowing the nature of these persons or their attitudes and abilities, one derives many clues concerning the nature of the project. If there are no other people involved in the question of the project, the one who asks the question is the person involved in the project. The present work covers projects and things much more fully and correctly than in the classic texts of King Wan and his son.

A few relevant keywords in describing anything has proved to be invaluable in most any subject of man's interest. For that reason I have added a brief glossary containing only the important keywords found in the delineation of the Hexagrams. Again, I stress the importance of memorizing the meanings of these words—not necessarily literally, but with a clear understanding so that their implications and applications are not forgotten.

KEY WORDS

Advantageous: In describing the auspiciousness of the figure, the King Wan text frequently uses this word in the sense of it being advantageous to be cautious and do nothing or to be advantageous in going forward to achievement. The text usually adds: "Under the *conditions* of the Hexagram."

Ancestors: In many of the Hexagrams there is reference to "going to the Ancestral Temple." In occidental thought, this means to try to get inspiration from the collective unconscious and perhaps from the subconscious. It implies that intellectual analysis is not enough.

Conditions: In describing the auspice of a Hexagram, the text states: "Fortunate under the conditions which this Hexagram denotes, or presupposes." For instance, if the Hexagram denotes the condition of "waiting," then the good fortune is limited to planning or consolidating one's project or position.

Crossing the Stream: This means to enlarge or to go beyond the natural sphere intended, to venture or advance confidently.

Daemon: One's Holy Guardian Angel, Higher Self, etc.—the supraconscious.

Firm and Correct: See Sincerity.

Great Stream: Expanded advancement beyond the normal sphere (see Line Positions).

Great One: To see or consult the Great One means to invoke the wisdom or aid of the supraconscious.

Heaven and Earth: Another term for Yang and Yin.

Hexagram: A figure consisting of two Trigrams. The lower Trigram conditions the ruling force and nature of the upper Trigram (see Trigrams).

Inferior/ Superior: The lower Trigram represents the inferior. The upper Trigram represents the superior. These descriptions may apply to one's own inferior and superior qualities or to another person.

Initiator: Starting energy and force. Represents Yang, to which its partner Yin responds and nourishes, develops and sustains the initial projecting force of Yang.

Khien: The Trigram with three Yang lines. Also referred to as Lingam. Khien is the Great Initiating Force.

Khwan: The Trigram of three Yin lines. Also referred to as Yoni. Khwan is the Great Womb, the nourisher and developer. Invokes and receives.

Line Positions: This is an important key in the Yi King.
    Marc Edmund Jones, an eminent authority on reformulated concepts in

astrology, wrote about the three Fire Signs—Aries, Leo and Sagittarius—in relation to their natural houses, the first, fifth and ninth, as follows: "The First House corresponds to *starting* a sphere. The Fifth House, to *attaining autocracy* in one's sphere. The Ninth House, to *going beyond one's sphere* or expanding it."

This concept has a remarkable correspondence with the three line positions. Line number one (the lowest) is symbolized as Earth and as being the human body *per se*, including the desires and emotional drives. Line number two—the central line—is the thinking man—the conscious mind. Line number three—the top line—is symbolized as "heaven"—superior-inspired wisdom.

Although in a Hexagram the upper three lines constitute the upper Trigram, the customary way of counting is to continue with four, five, and six lines. The upper Trigram is *superior* and the lower Trigram is *inferior.*

Sincerity: Implies self-honesty—knowing one's self to be ethical and honest in motive and action, firm and correct in both attitudes and methods.

Trigram: A figure which consists of a combination of three Yang or Yin lines. The Trigram represents the Cosmic Triad of body, mind, and soul (see Line Positions, Yang/Yin).

Yang/Yin: The cosmic principles of non-dualism, one of the keys to the "language" of the Yi King. Yang represents the male energy in all nature, and Yin is its complement, the female energy. They are co-equal and cooperating.

Wilhelm tries to make a point that these two words did not exist at the time of King Wan's writings. What did exist was the female, broken line and the male, whole line, which contained *all* the concepts now embodied in the words Yang and Yin. This amounts to the same type of ignorance that would be exhibited if one objected to the word *God* being used because it is a later word. The word in ancient Greece was *Theos*.

3 The Pristine Yi King Trigrams

*T*his treatise being an exposition of the original Yi King, it is necessary to give extensive attention to the eight Trigrams. This is something that has been given scant attention, both in the classical writings on the Yi and by occidental translators.

The entire structure of the Yi is based and built upon the eight Trigrams—the original Trigrams of Fu-Hsi. King Wan obscured their meaning by presenting them exactly opposite to the pattern of Fu-Hsi. It is the *logical* order of Fu-Hsi that is presented in Table 1 (page 25).

Fu-Hsi did not append one single word of explanation to these Trigrams. Probably he had disciples that were taught verbally. However, the astounding thing is that we do not need any written explanations.

The entire Yi King philosophy and cosmology can be reconstructed from the existing keys in these diagrams of the eight Pa Kua. It is only for convenience that I have presented the diagrammatic table to facilitate the reader's further study.

The first observation to make is the difference in the line structures: a whole line and a broken line. This presents the idea of the *duad*, which is basic in humanity's nature—whether it be a dualism of opposing forces or of cooperating partners.

The next observation concerns the three line positions. The recognition of the triad is also basic in humanity—consciously or unconsciously. The concept of Father-Mother-Son—*activity* working in *substance* to produce a *form*.

It is of little consequence to give all the tedious reasoning involved in determining the correspondences of the three line positions. Suffice it to say that the result was the same as indicated in the texts.

For example, we shall study the Trigram of Sun—number three.

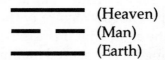

The central line is the conscious thinking and acting man. The line is a Yin, which means that he is receptive and invoking. The bottom line is Yang, which means his bodily equipment is "firm and correct," including the best of his instincts, emotions, and desires. All this Yang is projected in response to the central line of

#	Trigram	Symbol	Meaning	Quality	Sigil
1	☰	Heaven The Sky	Projecting Strength Power	Will Creation	Lingam T
2	☴	Wind Wood	Flexible Penetrating	Mind Image Concept	Air △
3	☲	Lightning Sun	Brightness Elegance	Realizing The Self	Sun ⊙
4	☶	Hills Mountains	Resting Arresting	Material Solidity The Body	Earth ▽
5	☱	Collected water Marsh/Lake	Pleasure Complacent Satisfied	Soul Pleasure Easy Move	Water ▽
6	☵	Rain Clouds	Peril Difficulty	Restricts	Moon ☽
7	☳	Thunder Lightning	Moving Exciting Power	Will	Fire △
8	☷	The Earth	Receptive Sustaining Nourishing	Expansion to Infinity	Yoni ◊

Table 1

receptivity and development. The soul powers of the upper line are projected to the receptive central line—Man. All of this agrees with the meaning given in the classic texts: brilliance, intelligence, realization—Sun. This Trigram of Sun is the most auspicious in a figure. Conversely, the Trigram of the Moon, being the opposite of the Sun Trigram, is the most inauspicious.

To illustrate this we shall study the Moon Trigram—number six.

The upper and lower lines are Yin and do *not* project. The lower line is the desires *wanting* to be satisfied. There is nothing of value given the man from his higher wisdom and direction, which is the central Yang line. He is beset with a drive for action, but there is nothing to support it from the other two lines. Therefore, the body, instincts, emotions, and desires give nothing much to the man—they are only asking to be filled up. The upper line offers nothing—there is no directive capacity. Compare this analysis of the lines of the Moon with the description given in the texts, in which it is symbolized as "a deep, wide gorge containing a torrent of water." It is essentially regarded as being restrictive—opposed to advancing—and even "perilous."

As a comparison to the above two figures, let us study the first Trigram, Khien.

In this figure all the lines are Yang, signifying greatness, the projective force, starting energy, initiative. There is no Yin line of response to receive, nourish, and sustain this energy. It is more of an abstraction, just as its opposite, Khwan, with its three Yin lines, is also an abstraction. It is the *union*, or cooperation, of these two great principles, Yin and Yang, that brings about the various *manifestations* of the other six Trigrams. Khien is the Great Originating Force and Khwan, the Womb of the Great Mother Earth, which receives and nourishes, supports and develops that which comes from the union with Khien. Thus, with the introduction of the first Yin line in Khien, we have the first response in number two, which is called Air. On the opposite side, the first Yang line of Khwan is the first manifested activity—called Fire or Thunder, meaning sudden, exciting energy.

There are four Trigrams that correspond with later concepts of the four Elements: Fire, Air, Water, and Earth. The Yi states number four to be a mountain having the same ideas of the fixed, stable, and solid qualities of Earth.

Number five is described as a placid body of water of "pleased satisfaction." (It is well named: Water.)

Number seven is described as thunder and lightning—"sudden, startling activity"—and is well symbolized as Fire.

Number two is Wind—"easily penetrating and penetrated," corresponding to the principle of Air.

It is not just coincidence that the opposite nature of Water and Earth are depicted with all lines being of opposite polarity—as are the lines of Air and Fire.

Thus we can see that even though Fu-Hsi left no written record of the eight Pa Kua, it is still possible to decipher its code and arrive at the same delineations of the eight Trigrams as stated in the two classic texts and early appendices. However, we admit that our examples of deduction are quite open to the fact that we have argued from the basis of first having taken the Trigram meanings from the texts and then making the deductions conform to those meanings.

In the next section we shall take the eight Trigram meanings, as admitted in the texts, and analyze each Hexagram based solely upon the two Trigrams and their position of upper or lower. In this process it is impossible to argue *ex post facto*, for we are bound by the stated meanings of the Trigrams. This method of deduction is meticulously observed in the extended delineations of the 64 Hexagrams in chapter 5.

Do the results prove that there is no such thing as a Hexagram *per se*, and that the Hexagram is, in fact, the combination of two Trigrams, of which there are 64 possible combinations? There is but one convincing proof. The implications of the combined two Trigrams determine the same general implications as delineated by King Wan and his son.

The meanings given by the Wans are in good agreement with the deduced Trigram method in 35 of the Hexagrams. They are in less than half agreement with 12 Hexagrams. There remain 15 more Hexagrams, which indicates that the Wans knew the correct meaning, but resorted to preaching metaphysical sermons because the Hexagrams were of such difficult or unfavorable augury. If this is true, then why did King Wan digress 15 times? We assume these were the occasions that he was giving moral encouragement to his followers or preaching. Those who do not know how to figure odds can be assured that the blind chance of arriving at this number of good agreements is only one in 167,772,480. The combined Trigram system is correct, and the Wans used the same system.

A good example of this is the number 42 Hexagram, which Wan named The Well—Moon over Air. He writes:

"Though the town may change for the worse, the central community well is still a sure and pure source of supply." The true meaning of this figure was surely in his mind when he referred to the unstable and upset conditions in a town. By naming the Hexagram The Well, he could expound optimistically on metaphysics. This again proves that he was reasoning from the combined Trigram system when he wrote about the Hexagram with the two referenced Trigrams *reversed:* i.e., Air over Moon, which he correctly describes as "Dissipation, Dispersion, Scattering of Values."

This example is enough to show one that it is not downgrading King Wan's perspicacity in the Yi when it becomes necessary to "correct" the several names he has given to 15 or more figures.

King Wan's son is different. He did more than writing after the manner of wise diviners. He often wrote in the manner that delighted the minds of the fortunetellers. There is much value in his writings, but one must know the value before recognizing it!

The Upper and Lower Positions

Many people have difficulty in understanding the significance and correspondences of the upper and lower positions of the Trigrams.

The upper Trigram is called the *superior* Trigram for the simple reason that, in relation to the question, it is either the controlling force or factor, or it *should* be. This controlling force may be oneself over an inferior (the lower position) or it may be another person. It might also mean the superior force of one's destiny or a self-created necessity which is the dominating force.

In any question where there are two or more people involved, the upper position relates to the person who is actually in the superior position. For example, when the subject is asking favors from one in a superior position, such as a boss, the boss is represented by the upper Trigram. In a man-woman relationship, the upper Trigram is the male position and the lower is the woman's position. This is the Yang and Yin energy. However, if the woman is in a superior position, for example, the boss, she is represented by the upper Trigram.

The upper position relates to dominance (or lack of it) that is "behind the scenes." Within a nation, the people vote, but that is not the rulership behind the scenes. The behind-the-scenes rulers are congress, kings, prime ministers, generals, queens, etc. This executive directive would amount to nothing without the multitudes (of the lower Trigram position) to carry it to objective manifestation. *This* is the implication of the lower position.

What, then, is the "name" of the behind-the-scenes directing capacity indicated by the upper Trigram position? One name will not satisfy all minds. Psychologist Jung called it his Daemon, and said that many times when he had previously decided upon a course of action he had been led into another course by his Daemon.

Let us also describe this "force" as a limited form of destiny. One may prefer to call it the direction of one's supraconscious mind. Let us simply say that it is some sort of condition behind the scenes which is to be carried out in some way by the person represented by the lower Trigram. The particular Trigram in the lower position describes the possible manner of carrying it out—or the inability to do so—and all of this is to be judged by whether it is in accord with it, against it, or indifferent to it. The same judgment occurs with the lower Trigram.

Here is a tricky point. If the upper Trigram is a "weak" or vulnerable Trigram in relation to the strong Trigram in the lower position, then it is still a dominating force—dominating to indicate difficulties or vulnerability consonant with the nature of the Trigram. Another important point: The upper Trigram may indicate one's Daemon, and according to the nature of the Trigram, the meaning will show either the support, neutrality, or prohibition of the Daemon.

In closing, there is a very good Chinese metaphorical illustration of the relationship between the upper and lower Trigrams: "Great indeed is the initiating energy of the Sun (Yang and upper position), but it would be nothing without the Earth (Yin and lower position) to nourish and develop it into manifestation."

The Eight Trigrams in the Upper Position

When number one Trigram Khien is over Khien, there is *great originating energy* but no place to go because there is no sustaining, responsive Yin line. On the other hand, when number eight Khwan is under Khien, all three lines are Yin. The great, strong energy of Khien is invoked by so much Yin that it is possible for Khien to waste too much energy on Khwan. But if the supplication of Khwan is not selfish and sensuous but is more idealistic (or even practical), then the portent is great for a good outcome.

Khien over number two Air is responsive, with the lowest line of Air being Yin. Khien is not invoked with much more than selfish or sensuous desires, so it is good only in small, insubstantial ways.

Khien over number three Sun has something worth its great initiating force. It combines marvelously with the Sun (brilliant realization) but is strictly a masculine Hexagram.

The greatness and force of Khien is restricted by

the lower Trigram of number four Earth. It would lend strength to consolidating material matters, but it is not good for advancement because Earth is fixed.

Khien over number five Water shows how the great energy and strength of Khien is dampened, but there can be great satisfaction—possibly too much of it, dampening any ambition.

Even the great Khien is frustrated and restricted by number six Moon in the lower position.

The great energy and creative will of Khien when conditioned by the lower number seven Fire (exciting emotional energy) requires intelligence and rectitude. However, with willing regulation it is of good augury.

One should always take note that when Khien is the upper Trigram, the Daemon is strong in reference to the project and is not acquiescent to foolishness or waywardness.

In number two Air, the lower line (Yin) indicates a lack of strength and instability in material manifestation. The second line, which represents the thinking man, and the third line, which represents the higher mind, are not supported by the material equipment and strength of the bottom line; therefore, the Trigram indicates the need for solid materialistic support.

For the foregoing reasons the Trigram is called Air and, as such, traditionally implies both *easily penetrated* and *easily penetrating*. For this reason and because the middle line represents the thinking person, this Trigram also represents the mind and mental activity.

Trigram number two Air in the upper position

represents anything (except material solidity) that is of very high class. The material solidity and support must be obtained from the four lower Trigrams that have a Yang lower line. These are Khien, Sun, Water, and Fire. A good simile is that the upper Trigram representing the knights and generals must depend on the support of the soldiers for carrying out the mental concepts, plans, and directives.

The best side of Air in the upper position is small restraint, free course, high mind, regulation and cooperation, imagination, responsiveness, uncontentiousness and great plans.

The weaker side is lack of support and cooperation from the lower Trigram, being subject to emotional impressions, and ameliorization if the ideals of the upper manifest to the lower and the lower responds in an unselfish way.

Idealistically it is good for seeking stability in conformity with certain plans and patterns.

With number three Sun in the upper position, we are to be ever reminded of the keyword meaning of this Trigram—*brilliant realization*. If the question is about some project, plan, or ideal, then brilliant realization is assured. It describes the superiority of the "superior" person in any question.

Metaphorically this Trigram is like the Sun at high noon or the Sun at its highest point in summer—in both cases brilliant realization at its peak.

High intelligence is implied in this Trigram when in the upper position—the intelligence given by both the higher instincts and the inspired wisdom of the supraconscious mind.

When number two Air is in the lower position, it indicates higher transformation—even alchemical transmutation, as in high sex magick.

With number four Earth there can be some restriction of the realized self (or project), but it could also indicate consolidation of the realization.

Number five Water in the lower position can be good if there is not too much egotistical satisfaction in the realizations.

With number six Moon there can be inability or incapacity—blindly struggling for realization. On the other hand, if the subject of the Moon intelligently seeks the wisdom of the Sun, he or she can profit thereby.

In the case of number seven Fire in the lower position, the natural, exciting movement of Fire requires self-discipline and sustained action to attain the best in realization.

There can be both accumulation and advance with number eight Khwan in the lower position if the "inferior" gives support to the upper instead of selfishly seeking the strength of the Sun.

Of all the eight Trigrams, Sun is the "gold." Gold has been the object of desire, greed, and robbery, but it need not be so if sincerity and aspiration can be invoked and there is no selfishness.

In number four Earth the keywords are *solidity* and *fixation*. The good aspects are soundness, stability, and consolidation. The unfavorable aspects are stubbornness, restriction, repression, and binding.

Whether the subject is a project, another person, one's own superior position with another, or even one's Daemon, the keywords of this Trigram in the upper position should be considered—in relation to the lower Trigram, of course.

This Trigram is also called Mountains, and when the lower Trigram is number six Moon, the texts state that "forbidding mountains challenge progress." On the other hand, when Khien is in the lower position, it is called "Giving great strength to the Grand Accumulation" (i.e., what has already been accumulated).

When the lower Trigram is number two Air, it is time to use the mind and make plans for maintaining stability. Physical force or aggressive methods are not very availing.

With number three Sun in the lower position, it is auspicious to make an outward show (called Ornament and Adornment) of one's realized accumulation—if not too ostentatious.

With number five Water in the lower position, stable, pleased satisfaction is indicated, but there is a diminishing of what one has in excess. It will bring increases in other ways—pleased satisfaction should be tempered with measured steps and patient regulation, or else restrictions.

With number seven Fire in the lower position, the exciting energy of this Trigram must be tempered with consideration and careful regulation of all the values and potentials to get the best from this augury. Contention in any fashion is futile.

The utmost expansion of "Earth" accumulation and solidity is found with number eight Khwan in the lower position. Everything is filled up and therefore no movement in any direction is advantageous—unless in anticipation of the beginning of a new cycle, considering that completion has been attained and that eventual change is needed.

Every line of the Trigram Water is of opposite polarity to the preceding Trigram Earth. The implications are also the opposite.

The keywords of number five Water are *pleasure* and *pleased satisfaction*, in which the "restriction" of Earth is anathema. Whether it be a project, another person, or one's own higher self, it is "complacent" to the conditions and movements indicated by the lower Trigram—except contention.

Number one Khien in the lower position challenges inordinate pleased satisfaction and demands some energy and action, but with good results.

Number two Air is penetrative and seeks action, and there is some indication that Water may be hesitant in acting out the requirements, even though having them. Good for stirring some ambition in number five Water.

Number three Sun can bring satisfaction to Water—even to the point of surfeit—and produce change.

Number four Earth brings a practical and consolidating influence upon the complacency of Water with good, practical mutual influence.

Number six Moon brings either incompetence or no desire for any worthwhile attainment or growth. This is not a good augury.

With number seven Fire in the lower position, ideally there is a reconciliation of the exciting energy of Fire and the easygoing complacency of Water, but it can be a delicate balance if there is any contention.

With number eight Khwan in the lower Trigram there is great capacity, nourishment, and growth. Good things are collected together.

Life cannot, or should not, be a continuous striving, and number five Water is that part of the cycle where there is the blessing of pleasure and satisfaction in preparation for the beginning of a new cycle.

The key idea of number six Moon is more ambition or drive than required ability or practical potential. Whether the Moon position represents another person, one's self, or one's higher self, the key idea implies what King Wan described as "peril, hazardous difficulty."

There is only one Trigram in the lower position that gives promise to a really good augury—number three Sun. The corresponding lines of the Sun and Moon are of opposite polarity. When number three Sun is in the lower position, there is promise of realization if attention is placed on completion and consolidation of the past in accord with the present and near future.

If the person recognizes what is good about the

implications of the upper Trigram (Moon) and is willing to give unstinting support to same (in union and harmony), then there can be a good outcome—but it is an IF.

With number one Khien in the lower position there is great impulse for starting action, but the advice is to wait for a better sign.

With number two Air in the lower Trigram there are upset conditions but an element of hope for the future.

When number four Earth is in the lower position, let discreet movement alternate with discreet inactivity—do not push hard.

It is advised to suppress rising desires for pleased satisfaction when number five Water is in the lower Trigram.

Number seven Fire indicates the strivings and difficulties of the first stage of growth—but expect no long-term, static security.

Number seven Fire is well described as the sudden, exciting activity and force of thunder and lightning. Typically it is not a planned activity, but rather an almost blind force that is instinctive to some extent.

With number one Khien in the lower position there is great strength and vigor, but it needs purposeful direction. Avoid violent action and contention.

There is good movement and easy penetration if number two Air (mind) is assisting number seven Fire (will).

With the Sun (number three) in the lower position, there is the promise of full realization of the upper Trigram (energy and will).

When number four Earth is in the lower Trigram position, the energy of Fire is only partly restricted by Earth. It is an excellent indication for forming a foundation for future action and good fortune. The stimulus of Fire gives good mobility to materialistic Earth, transcending materialistic selfishness.

With number five Water in the lower Trigram, there is most likely an excessive desire for sensual satisfaction. However, when directed by virtue, correctness, and less concern for pleasure, it could be auspicious in bringing higher pleased satisfaction.

Number six Moon in the lower position indicates that there are knots and complications to unravel or that it is expedient to retire and wait.

With number eight Khwan in the lower position there is great responsive desire and capacity for nourishing, supporting, and developing what has been initiated by Fire.

No matter which Trigram is in the lower position, the Fire Trigram in the upper position requires some intelligent and purposeful direction from the subject of the lower position.

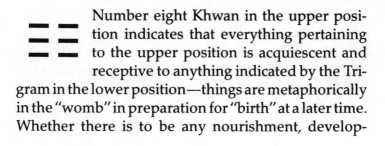 Number eight Khwan in the upper position indicates that everything pertaining to the upper position is acquiescent and receptive to anything indicated by the Trigram in the lower position—things are metaphorically in the "womb" in preparation for "birth" at a later time. Whether there is to be any nourishment, develop-

ment, or physical manifestation depends upon not only the nature of the lower Trigram but also whether there is sincere and willing cooperation with the upper.

In this respect, if number six Moon is the lower Trigram, there is an overambitious, incompetent "inferior" bringing little that is worthwhile; on the other hand, with number three Sun in the lower position, there is more promise for attaining realization, and with sincerity and worthy aims an excellent outcome is the augury.

With number one Khien in the lower position it is suggested that the "superior" (Khwan) is submissive and nourishing in allowing the materialistic lower to have dominant force and energy and free play. If deserving of this, then it is excellent.

Number two Air in the lower indicates advancing upward in aspiration, but no material solidity. It is excellent for making plans.

Just remain still and disciplined with number four Earth in the lower position. Stability is forming, but only for a future date.

With number five Water in the lower position there is no material gain, only the expansion of pleased satisfaction.

Number seven Fire in the lower position indicates free course and development; in other words, there is some danger of blind, misdirected, unintelligent energy.

The Eight Trigrams in the Lower Position

With number one Khien under number two Air, there are great ambitions, free course, and quick, easy successes or advances but not on a grand scale.

With Khien under number three Sun, there is great energy to secure and make strong accumulated realizations. The lower Trigram can be a great help to the upper in thinking things out.

With Khien under Earth, number four, the fixedness of Earth is stirred up. Khien gives the necessary strength and force to material resources.

Number one Khien under number five Water indicates that pleased satisfaction receives some needed impetus of activity and strength. The advice is not to contend with the desire for pleased satisfaction.

Khien under number seven Fire indicates an abundance of great vigor and activity. The lower Trigram can temper the unthinking, sudden action implied by the upper Trigram.

With Khien under number eight Khwan, the upper Trigram is completely complacent to whatever activity is initiated by Khien, and therefore unwarranted initiating force may bring contention at a future time. In man/woman relationships, the polarities are reversed from the norm. There are cases where this would mean a good augury. In the indications of this Hexagram, care should be taken that the subjects of the lower Trigram be moderate in using great energy and force.

As mentioned before, the Trigram of Air always implies easy penetration and being easily penetrated—such is the quality of "air." This Trigram also relates to mental activity. In this case, with a Yin line in the lowest position, the emotional desires yearn to be filled and satisfied. The two upper lines, which are Yang, imply a fine mind and even inspired wisdom—the weakness being desire.

With number four Earth, number five Water, and number six Moon over Air, unfavorable influences exist. With Earth, a solution of constricted and tangled material conditions is necessary, but not easily accomplished. Air under Water indicates incongruous conditions and small, worthy ambitions—a weak bridge to walk. Under Moon there are unstable conditions, and only well-planned action can help.

With Air under number one Khien, great progress and success is indicated in a variety of actions and endeavors. Because of the nature of Air, duration or stability is not assured. The danger lies in frittering away one's interests in small, unworthy activities. Some planned direction is well advised.

Number two Air under number seven Fire is also a positive Hexagram. The mind works with the will, but for a positive outcome one must act out the laws of one's own being. As with the preceding Hexagram, the correct aim and procedure must be maintained.

With Air under number three Sun, from the standpoint of transcendental Magick, the greatest of the 64 Hexagrams is indicated. It is both the Great Transformer and alchemical transmutation. It is *the* great auspice for self-transcendence in alchemical sex magick.

Great progress and success brought to realization is indicated.

For all general purposes, number three Sun can be classed as the "best" Trigram and its opposite, number six Moon, the "worst." Each corresponding line of Sun and Moon are of opposite polarity—Yang vs. Yin.

The bottom line of Sun, being Yang, indicates strong, good instincts, desires, and materialistic ambitions, as well as a strong, correct working person. The top Yang line shows strong, correct aspirations and inspiration—even an unconscious wisdom. The central line always indicates the thinking, self-directed person. With this line being Yin, it indicates that it is completely receptive to the good shown in the upper and lower lines. The result of this is good or brilliant realization—constructive success. Number six Moon, on the other hand, indicates more drive and ambition than existing ability.

With number three Sun under number one Khien, there is much concerted masculine drive for progress and success. This is a very energetic Hexagram. The Chinese call it the Union of Men.

Sun under number eight Khwan indicates that everything (and every person) is receptive to the drive of the Sun for realization, and will, in many ways, give great support, even invisible support.

In relation to Trigrams number two Air, number four Earth, number five Water, and number seven Fire, Sun creates very good, strong and satisfactory combinations, but in conformity with the nature of the particular upper Trigram. Even under the "bad" number six Moon, Sun is good for consolidating and completing the present and the past. Generally, the Sun Trigram in the lower position indicates superiority over the subject of the upper Trigram.

The Earth Trigram, number four, is comparable to all living things (including humans) in Nature that have the instinct for security and the desire to be impregnable to the encroachment of outside or alien forces. It is the most materialistic of the Trigrams and is also very self-centered.

The best of Earth is stability, consolidation, physical strength, and practicality. The worst is stubbornness to change and restriction.

When Earth is under number one Khien, there is growth and increase in the power of the lower Trigram. It cooperates with the upper only if there is material benefit, but then it becomes very willing.

With Earth under number two Air, slow, gradual advance is indicated. There is stability with fixed patterns, plans, and conditions.

Earth under number three Sun brings the image of the realized self which is restricted to material or practical matters.

When Earth is under number five Water, practical materialism is tempered with complacency and pleasure. There is mutual influence between both upper and lower; no contention.

Earth under number six Moon shows difficulty

and incompetence. The best course of action to follow is to advance by small movements alternating with discreet inactivity.

Earth under number seven Fire indicates limited advancement and success. It is good for forming a basis for future action.

Under number eight Khwan, Earth gets great support, but not beyond one's own natural sphere. It is of good augury. This is a consolidation in "matter" (and the practical) of natural advantageous desires. The upper is helpful to the good desires of the lower.

The number five Trigram Water is supposed to be envisioned as the placid water of a lake. The keywords are *pleasure* and *pleased satisfaction*. The two lower lines are strong, active, Yang lines. This indicates that despite the placidity implied by "water," there is a strong drive behind the desire for pleased satisfaction. Under certain circumstances, this can lead to oversensuality.

With Water under Khien, it is auspicious even if under great activity and drive for satisfaction and complacency.

Under number two Air, the "superior" condescends and the "inferior" responds. Lack of stability requires deliberation. This is the Great Hexagram for imagination in the truest magickal sense.

With Water under number three Sun, realization is attained by easy, pleasurable methods and conditions. It is a good augury for self-transcendence.

Water under number four Earth requires measured steps, patient stability, and regulation for the greatest material satisfaction.

Water under number six Moon indicates restricted satisfaction. The best course is to suppress overly ambitious desires.

Water under number seven Fire indicates too much sudden emotional activity, and unless the action derives from good plans, there is disparity.

With Water in the lower position to number eight Khwan, the upper is willing to give large support and development to what is good in the desire for pleased satisfaction. This is generally a good augury, especially if the lower acts out the indications of submitting to the higher authority of the "superior."

The metaphysical keywords of number six Moon are *youthful inability and inexperience*. The following illustration is metaphorical. The bottom line of Moon represents the instincts, emotions, and physical equipment of a twelve-year-old. The drive for self-direction, growth, and attainment represented by the middle Yang line is as strong as that of a twenty-year-old. The upper line being Yin indicates both the lack of higher direction which is born of much digested experience and the lack of aspiration to the wisdom of the Higher Self.

Therefore, when we consider that the actual carrying out of any project is represented by the lower Trigram, the Moon in this position indicates inability and inexperience no matter what the upper Trigram is. If the question refers to the relation of oneself with another person (or persons), then the same indications apply for the "inferior." If the "superior" Trigram is represented by number one Khien or number three

Sun, this indicates that there can be some good augury IF the "inferior" seeks aid and cooperation from the "superior."

With Moon under number seven Fire, there is a good chance for removing obstacles.

Under number eight Khwan, there is a willing help of giving nourishment and growth to the lower Trigram if there is good purpose involved.

Moon under number three Sun is almost always good if the question involves a man/woman relationship.

Under number two Air, there is a scattering of values or dissipation. With good intent, it is good for mental activities, and with Moon under number four Earth, it is good for mental concentration.

General advice for all cases is to wait for a more auspicious time or set of conditions. Take no great action.

Number seven Fire in the lower position is symbolized by lightning—sudden, exciting, active force and energy. It derives from the emotions and instincts and has no conscious, planned direction. It is a simple drive to start action from an inactive condition.

With Fire under number one Khien, there is GREAT exciting motive and initiating power and activity. This is more intelligently directed than in the simple Fire Trigram, but is still inclined to go to many small things. Rectitude, planning, and self-control are essential for anything of great value. It is much the same when under Trigram number two Air, except that there is great energy given to the mind.

With number three Sun in the upper position, the

lower must look to the "superior" for inspiration and motivation. It gives continuous activity to the realization implied by Sun.

While the subject of number four Earth may need some stirring up by Fire, some temperate regulation is required to bring about consolidation of things.

With Fire under number five Water, there can be a reconciliation between the complacency of Water and the demand for action of Fire, but it requires concern and effort. Complacency needs a bit of stirring up!

Fire under number six Moon brings an unfavorable augury and hazards.

Fire in the lower position is the first stirring activity that stimulates the completely Yin Trigram of number eight Khwan, and it is welcomed and supported. The "inferior" Fire has great free course and support from the "superior" Khwan. The only obstacle can be unworthy or misdirected energy.

The keywords of Khwan are *great receptiveness* with respect to Yang initiative, with great capacity for support and development to that which is initiated by Yang force. When both Trigrams are Khwan, there is nothing to develop.

Under number one Khien, Khwan invokes the "superior" Khien to the great advantage of both. If the subject of Khwan is not too self-seeking, the cooperation is ideal. This is the best auspice for man/woman relationships.

Under number two Air, Khwan gives great expansion and development to the mental concept of Air.

With number three Sun, both "superior" and "inferior" advance and accumulate in realization. Khwan looks up to Sun. This is excellent for man/woman relationships.

Under number four Earth, the expansion of materialism and fixedness is taken to the limit. There is no progress.

With number five Water in the upper position, both Trigrams are in agreement for advancement and development of pleased satisfaction (sensual).

If the "inferior" Khwan submits to the "superior" Moon without reservation, there is no good augury.

Under number seven Fire, Khwan has great desire and capacity for development in response to the awakening energy of Fire.

With number eight Khwan in the upper position, the Trigram of Khwan is doubled. With no Yang lines, this is metaphorically the unimpregnated womb.

4 Determining the Hexagram

*I*n their initial purity, the Trigrams are evolved thus:

3rd line: —— —— —— —— — — — — — — — —
2nd line: —— —— — — — —
1st line: —— — —

One line divides and makes two; the two divide and make four; the four divide and make eight. Since this is a logical order, we always start building from the *base* of the figure. All *lower* Trigrams are evolved by going **across** the page. All *upper* Trigrams are evolved by going **down** the page (refer to Table 2).

For example, to find Sun of Sun, check the Trigram of Sun, which is number three. Then follow this column down to the Sun Trigram of the downward column. The result will be Hexagram number 19 of the logical order.

Moon of Fire consists of the number six Trigram (across) and the number seven Trigram (down). Following the same procedure as in the above example, we find it to be in the number 54 square, which is the Hexagram number 54.

The main requirement is to memorize the order of the Trigrams so that, in time, the table will not have to be used as a reference. One aid is to note that the Yang line is the upper line for the first four Trigrams and that the Yin line is the upper line in the next four Trigrams. On the Yang side, the first change of polarity is the bottom line, which changes to Yin. On the Yin side, the first change from Khwan is the bottom line changing to Yang.

It is always well to check the structure of the Hexagram against the combination of the two Trigrams. In that way, there is no possibility of deriving the wrong figure.

The Logical Square

In the delineations of the Hexagrams given in Table 3, the number is placed on the left side of the figure. The other number, appearing on the right side in parentheses, is the number given by King Wan and is used in the texts of Legge and Wilhelm. It is included here in the event you may wish to refer to the other translations.

Changing the number does not affect the nature of the Hexagram. The Hexagram remains the same. Only the number of it is different from that of the logical order.

LOWER TRIGRAM / UPPER TRIGRAM	T (1)	△ (2)	⊙ (3)	▽ (4)	▽ (5)	☽ (6)	△ (7)	◯ (8)
T (1)	1	2	3	4	5	6	7	8
△ (2)	9	10	11	12	13	14	15	16
⊙ (3)	17	18	19	20	21	22	23	24
▽ (4)	25	26	27	28	29	30	31	32
▽ (5)	33	34	35	36	37	38	39	40
☽ (6)	41	42	43	44	45	46	47	48
△ (7)	49	50	51	52	53	54	55	56
◯ (8)	57	58	59	60	61	62	63	64

Table 2
Derivation of the Hexagrams

The Sigils

For the sake of convenience it is well to memorize these sigils, which constitute the quality or element of each Trigram.

Element	Sigil
(1) Khien or Lingam	T
(2) Air	△
(3) Sun	⊙
(4) Earth	▽
(5) Water	▽̶
(6) Moon	☽
(7) Fire	△
(8) Khwan or Yoni	◊

Casting the Hexagram

By using the Ho River Map system, Wilhelm may have presented one of the greatest methods of divination in existence, but it is not the *pure* Yi. This present treatise is devoted to presenting the Pristine Yi. There is no numerology involved in either erecting or interpreting the Hexagram. We are therefore obliged to pass by the method of the 49 stalks of the divining plant for three reasons: (1) it is a contrived numerology, (2) the method is described ambiguously, and (3) there is reason to deduce that any authentic method was kept secret and not fully given in writing.

1 (1)	2 (44)	3 (13)	4 (33)	5 (10)	6 (6)	7 (25)	8 (12)
9 (9)	10 (57)	11 (37)	12 (53)	13 (61)	14 (59)	15 (42)	16 (20)
17 (14)	18 (50)	19 (30)	20 (56)	21 (38)	22 (64)	23 (21)	24 (35)
25 (26)	26 (18)	27 (22)	28 (52)	29 (41)	30 (4)	31 (27)	32 (23)
33 (43)	34 (28)	35 (49)	36 (31)	37 (58)	38 (47)	39 (17)	40 (45)
41 (5)	42 (48)	43 (63)	44 (39)	45 (60)	46 (29)	47 (3)	48 (8)
49 (34)	50 (32)	51 (55)	52 (6)	53 (54)	54 (40)	55 (51)	56 (16)
57 (11)	58 (46)	59 (36)	60 (15)	61 (19)	62 (7)	63 (24)	64 (12)

Table 3
The Logical Square

In conclusion, if there had been any recognized authenticity in this involved numerology method, then King Wan's son, in his account of the six line positions, would have revealed his recognition of it.

It was in the early 1940s that I was talking with an aged Chinese sage about the Yi King. We discussed the possibility of erecting the oracular Hexagram. We both agreed that the oracle should be determined not by blind chance, but that the supraconscious should be uppermost in making a casting. Due to my insistence, I was invited to be initiated into the *Order of the Singing Fan*—a most secret Order claiming uninterrupted existence from before the time of King Wan. Two years later, this venerable sage proclaimed that within the next 15 years, he and all other members of the *Singing Fan* would be "with their ancestors," and the doors would be closed to the Order. He agreed that some of the secrets of this Order should be put in print for the first time. The primary secrets were the three methods of erecting a Hexagram.

The Method of the Dice

On a table before the operator, place one die on the right side with the number one facing upwards. On the left side place the other die with the number six facing upwards.

Touch the number one die with the fingers—keep them in constant contact with the die. Then, without looking, turn the die over in different directions until impelled to stop. If the number on top is an *odd* number, it is Yang. This is recorded as the *bottom* line.

With the left hand, repeat the process. Again, the odd or even number determines it to be either Yang or Yin. This is line two.

Reset the dice again: one and six facing upwards. Repeat the operation, which then gives lines three and four. Another repetition completes lines five and six.

Primarily, that supra-"something" has been responsible in determining the Hexagram. This is quite different from *throwing* dice down and depending on blind chance.

It is interesting to note the extraordinary correspondence between the *cube* and the Yi. There are eight corners on the cube that correspond to the eight Trigrams. There are six faces of the cube to correspond to the six lines of the Hexagram. There are 12 edges to correspond to the possible two polarities of each line. There are three edges converging to a point to correspond with the three lines of the Trigram. Thus, the entire eight Trigrams can be diagrammed on the cube.

In working with this method of placing the fingers on the dice, be careful not to let the fingers leave contact with the cube when determining a line. This allows the supraconscious to operate. A short, sincere ritual before erecting the Hexagram provides help in attaining that state known as ESP, and it is this sensitivity that will prompt the moment to lift your fingers from the cube.

This method may not be so very secret, as the two cubes (or dice) have been used in this and many other ways. However, the following two methods, the Chess and the Time methods, are of unique value. These latter methods have never before been even remotely approximated in print.

The Chess Method

The 64 Hexagrams correspond to the 64 squares of the chessboard, and the six different chess pieces correspond to the six line positions in the Hexagram—this can hardly be coincidence.

The Correspondences
Line positions from bottom to top

Chess	Yi King	Symbolic Meaning
6 Pawns	The multitude; foot soldiers	The type of desires, emotions, instincts, of the "common people." Materialistic. Lacking intelligent self-direction.
2 Knights	Knights and minor generals	Having some intelligent self-direction—not common followers. Thinking man instead of the lowly.
2 Bishops	Priests, Scribes, Advisers	Looks and aspires to something higher than self, i.e., to at least some self-transcendence.
2 Rooks	Feudal Princes	Practical wisdom. Ideally, supports the high aims of humanity. Also good executive ability, supporter to the Highest in Man, yet also can be a hard "Enforcer."
King	Ruler	The High Ruler of the Hexagram—or should be. Inspired Greatness—also the Daemon.
Queen	The Great Sage/ The Great Womb of Heaven	The Great Invisible, Intangible Rulership. The Great Repository of self-created necessity and destiny.

Refer to the Logical Square diagram (Table 3). That vertical row of squares which contains the eight Hexagrams that have number one (Khien) for the lower Trigram is the side of the board for the *white* pieces. The vertical row that has number eight (Khwan) as the lower Trigram for all the eight Hexagrams is the side of the board for the *black* pieces.

When making a chess move with a white piece, sit on the side of the board belonging to white. When making a move from the black side, merely turn the board around so that it correctly faces you. No matter from which side you play, you are playing in opposition to another. This is important. Do not favor one side or the other.

If playing alone, the game could last too long. In order to prevent this, you should remove some identical pieces from both sides so as to shorten the game.

For those who do not know how to play chess, he or she can learn the proper arrangement of the pieces and their moves in less than a half hour. It is very well worth it.

As in standard chess, the game is concluded when either the white or the black King piece has been checkmated. The square held by the piece that checkmates the King is the oracular Hexagram to your question, and its number can be determined by referring to the table of the 64 Hexagrams!

There is yet even more to this. The square being held by the checkmated King gives the Hexagram an indication of how and where your project or other person is most vulnerable.

By way of example: Suppose the question is about

the success or growth of some project, and the check-mated King was on the square called Great Havings. You may ask how this could possibly be a point of vulnerability in your project. It could be either an idea to dispose of some of those "havings," or a stubborn determination to accumulate great havings. In either case, it could define your *vulnerability* in lieu of the major oracular Hexagram figure.

In answer to the question, What is so good about this chess game method? the answer is clear and definitive. Your supraconsciousness has had a chance to participate in the operation, thereby giving you a correct Hexagram instead of a haphazard one. You do not have to read anything *into* the Hexagram to get the answer. Often, this reading *into* or *out of* the meaning of the figure requires a very special gift.

The Time Method or Significant Hour

For years I had spent many sleepless nights cogitating on the problem of the order of the Trigrams around a circle. When this was finally solved, the *Singing Fan*, in recognition of my plight, gave me the Hour Table of the entire 64 Hexagrams. This is actually an extension of the order of the eight Trigrams.

The Fu-Hsi order of the Trigrams, when in a straight line, is clear enough. But there is another involved factor when they are arranged in a circle. In one sequence the top line must always be Yang, while in the other sequence Yin is always on top.

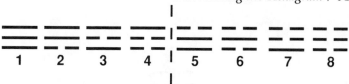

The first four Trigrams have a Yang upper line. The other four have a Yin upper line. Note that on the Yang side, the Yin begins to progress from the bottom and work upwards, until only the top line remains Yang. On the Yin side, we must work backwards from eight to five, and then we see the Yang lines progressing from the bottom, until in number five there is only one Yin line: the top one. This is the key for arranging the Trigrams in a circle (see illustration on page 62).

In this circular arrangement, King Wan and his son included some compass directions corresponding to the various Yi figures. This has nothing to do with the pure Yi. The circular arrangement applies to the *time* element involved in the changing relationship of the Earth moving around the Sun.

In this diagram, the vertical line bisects the sphere in two equal parts. At the bottom is number three (Sun), which marks midsummer, midday, and high noon. At the opposite point is number six (Moon) marking midwinter and midnight.

In astrology, this Earth-sphere is divided into 12 equal parts, designated as houses. In the Yi we have eight equal divisions, and you will note that when the hemisphere is divided into two parts (at right angles), number one (Khien or Lingam) indicates the time of both the Vernal Equinox and a theoretical sunrise. Number eight (Khwan, or Yoni) indicates the time of the Autumnal Equinox and a theoretical sunset.

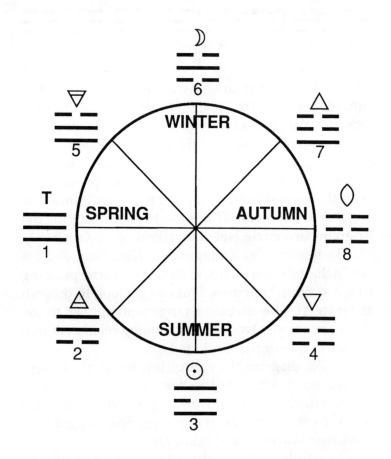

The Timetable of the Eight Trigrams

(1) Khien: 6 A.M. to 9 A.M.   (2) Air: 9 A.M. to noon
(3) Sun: Noon to 3 P.M.   (4) Earth: 3 P.M. to 6 P.M.
(8) Khwan: 6 P.M. to 9 P.M.   (7) Fire: 9 P.M. to midnight
(6) Moon: Midnight to 3 A.M.   (5) Water: 3 A.M. to 6 P.M.

Timetable of the 64 Hexagrams

The first 16 Hexagrams are for the morning hours:

Hex.	Hour	Hex.	Hour
1	6:00 to 6:23	9	9:00 to 9:23
2	6:23 to 6:45	10	9:23 to 9:45
3	6:45 to 7:08	11	9:45 to 10:08
4	7:08 to 7:30	12	10:08 to 10:30
5	7:30 to 7:53	13	10:30 to 10:53
6	7:53 to 8:15	14	10:53 to 11:15
7	8:15 to 8:38	15	11:15 to 11:38
8	8:38 to 9:00	16	11:38 to 12:00

The following 16 Hexagrams are for the evening hours:

17	12:00 to 12:23	25	3:00 to 3:23
18	12:23 to 12:45	26	3:23 to 3:45
19	12:45 to 1:08	27	3:45 to 4:08
20	1:08 to 1:30	28	4:08 to 4:30
21	1:30 to 1:53	29	4:30 to 4:53
22	1:53 to 2:15	30	4:53 to 5:15
23	2:15 to 2:38	31	5:15 to 5:38
24	2:38 to 3:00	32	5:38 to 6:00

Take careful note: From this point of Big Khwan, the four major Trigrams and the 32 Hexagrams proceed backwards from the logical order, until returning to Big Khien.

Evening to midnight:

Hex.	Hour	Hex.	Hour
64	6:00 to 6:23	56	9:00 to 9:23
63	6:23 to 6:45	55	9:23 to 9:45
62	6:45 to 7:08	54	9:45 to 10:08
61	7:08 to 7:30	53	10:08 to 10:30
60	7:30 to 7:53	52	10:30 to 10:53
59	7:53 to 8:15	51	10:53 to 11:15
58	8:15 to 8:38	50	11:15 to 11:38
57	8:38 to 9:00	49	11:38 to 12:00 A.M.

Midnight to morning:

Hex.	Hour	Hex.	Hour
48	12:00 to 12:23	40	3:00 to 3:23
47	12:23 to 12:45	39	3:23 to 3:45
46	12:45 to 1:08	38	3:45 to 4:08
45	1:08 to 1:30	37	4:08 to 4:30
44	1:30 to 1:53	36	4:30 to 4:53
43	1:53 to 2:15	35	4:53 to 5:15
42	2:15 to 2:38	34	5:15 to 5:38
41	2:38 to 3:00	33	5:38 to 6:00

Casting a Hexagram by this method is much like casting a horary chart in astrology. The exact minute of time is most important and necessary in making such a calculation. This foregoing timetable has never before been in print. There are two specific rules to follow:

1. Note the time the question is asked. Refer to the Hexagram that corresponds to the time. This is your oracular Hexagram. If the question comes to you late at night, jot down the time for future reference.

2. In dealing with another person, select an appropriate Hexagram. Then bring up the subject when the Hexagram time is in force. In this way you should eventually notice the differences as the time moves from one Hexagram to another!

If daylight saving time is in force, there must be a one-hour correction. Clock time is correct only if you are living on one of the standard meridians, i.e., the 75, 90, 105 or 120 meridian. For example: If you are living four degrees *east* of the standard meridian, the correction is five minutes for each degree from the meridian. Five minutes times four degrees is 20 minutes correction to be added to your local time.

If the locality is *west* of the time meridian, then the 20 minutes difference is subtracted from your clock time.

Other Suggested Methods for Casting the Hexagram

1. Slowly pace a circle and when impelled, stop. If the left foot is forward, it is a Yin Line; if the right foot is forward, a Yang line. Repeat until the six lines are completed.

2. Concentrate. Try to visualize a Trigram in your mind's eye. This will be the lower Trigram. Repeat for the upper Trigram.

3. Concentrate on the question. Let your index finger slowly move around over the table of the 64 Hexagrams. Stop on one when you have a strong impulse to stop. That is your Hexagram. (Important note: You can see that these Hexagrams are not arrived

at by blind chance. Your actions should be the result of your higher unconscious *Intelligence* having had a chance to determine the Hexagram.

An important reminder: Do not try to read into the Hexagram any conclusions that have not been included in your question. When you want further guidance on the subject you simply put another question to the Yi and make another Hexagram. You may put as many questions as you want to the Yi on various aspects of your object of inquiry, but *never* ask the same question twice. Aleister Crowley, probably the most persistent consultant of the Yi, has frequently put as many as six different questions to the Yi, all relating to the main question but never identical.

5 Interpretations of the 64 Yi Figures

The very first thing that one should do in interpreting the Hexagrams is to realize that every answer is limited to the precise question that has been asked. In the King Wan text, and in almost all of the 64 figures that he interprets, he states, "Under the conditions that are presupposed." This simply means, "Strictly under the conditions of the question that has been put to the Yi." One must not read any interpretation into the figure that is not restricted to the question. A sloppy question brings a sloppy answer. (Note: Never insult the intelligence of the Yi by asking the same question twice. However, one may ask as many as a dozen *different* questions that are relevant to the subject.)

Included with the following interpretations of

each of the 64 figures is the interpretation of King Wan (upon which all other translations are based). There are three reasons for this:

1. There are going to be those who, in seeking the answer to any particular question, will consult both this text and the other works based on the work of King Wan. This will save you the trouble of having to refer to another book.

2. The reader will then see why King Wan did not give true interpretations to several of the figures and why the interpretations based on the Pristine Yi are correct.

3. It helps to prepare one to follow the method of any real astrologer, which is to interpret the meaning and significance without slavishly referring to a book. This is the great value of being guided by the original Pristine Yi, which was not even set to print.

It bears repetition that one should keep in mind that the upper Trigram position is the significator of the invisible influence or power (or lack of it). In the Wan & Son texts there are various references to the Daemon, such as the King, the Queen, the Great One, and even "time to ascend the stairs to the Ancestral Temple." For years, I have racked my brains on how to frame one or two sentences, in plain words, that would define the nature of the Daemon. Finally, the following came to mind:

There is a natural psychological force which operates in accordance with one's *self-created necessity*

—either in help and superior guidance, in necessary restriction, or in simple acquiescence.

With this in mind, let one take heed of this influence in the description of the following 64 figures.

1 (1) KHIEN

Lingam of Lingam

"Great and originating. Penetrating. Firm and correct. Activity. Advantageous."

There is no Yin principle in this figure, and therefore nothing is to be received, nourished, or developed in that which has been originated or started.

If one is "firm and correct" it is auspicious for originating or initiating something. But note the injunction of the text, which says: "It is not the time for active doing"—i.e., it is excellent for both planning and setting into motion the activity, but response and development must await the future.

It may be generally implied that when initiated with firmness and correctness, there is a result; but the

Hexagram does not guarantee great responsive results (refer to the opposite figure, number 64—Khwan of Khwan).

There is a warning in this Hexagram to not exceed the proper limits of activity. It warns against blind, uncontrolled, or misdirected activity and energy. It is not good for a man/woman relationship.

The text correctly stresses that "It is advantageous to meet with the Great Man." In fact, it is advisable to aspire to wisdom or high counsel. There is an obscure reference in an appendix that this Hexagram is the "great transformer"—which should also be given greater consideration.

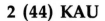

2 (44) KAU

Air of Lingam

"Suddenly meeting a bold woman, but do not associate with her for a long time and do not wed her."

Symbolically, this would also mean not to allow low people to have influence in one's affairs—to keep one's flighty desires and emotions within a reasonable boundary.

Since the upper five lines are strong Yang, it should not be difficult for any "correct" person to overrule the adverse force of line one. But there is another side to this: The emotions, desires, and active instincts of line one receive the great force and energy of the upper five Yang lines, and this is therefore very active and strong. It is enough to say, "Do not associate too long or too seriously."

The Trigram of Air is the mental image of Khien, or what is great. Therefore, there is some urge to self-transcendence in line one, and it would not be entirely correct to look down upon line one.

The Air Trigram means "easily penetrating" and "easily penetrated." If this fits in with what would be desirable in the question or subject involved, it is clear that this Hexagram is of better auspice than the implications in the texts. However, in some questions, easy penetration and easy penetrability imply warnings.

This is a most excellent Hexagram for the "superior" to uplift the "inferior" one. Man/woman relationships may be either good or superficial, depending upon "the firm and correct."

3 (13) THUNG ZAN

Sun of Lingam

The text, without coherent cause, calls this Hexagram "Union of Men." The only specific union that can be deduced from this figure is that the thinking, intelligent man of line two and what the text calls the "superior man of wisdom" of line five are in mutual response. This also advises that it is auspicious to aspire to the union with one's Divine Genius, as well as seek the help and wisdom and force of the "superior man."

The meaning is clear. The Trigram of Sun is "brilliance and realization of Khien, the Great." The text rightly states: "It will be advantageous to cross the Great Stream," and also, "advantageous to maintain the firm correctness of the superior man."

In this Hexagram the two sides of the Leo person are well described: (1) the truly kingly or queenly person, and (2) the insufferable, self-assertive superior one, who demands subservience rather than respect.

This is an excellent figure for *invoking* the wisdom, guidance, and help of one's Superior Genius—the Great One. Also, for asking favors of "superiors." If it be a "true" Hexagram, it implies realization, brilliance, or the realized self.

Man/woman relationships: If the firm correctness of the superior man is maintained and there is real aspiration in the woman, then it is excellent. But without this, there is apt to be "occasion for regret."

4 (33) THUN

Earth of Lingam

"Retiring Tail."
"There is a large growth of small men before whose advance superior men must retire. Small men multiply and increase in power."

This is a fair, though partial, picture of the Hexagram, despite the fact that the Wans arrived at this conclusion from a false premise. They considered this Hexagram to represent being in the grip of winter. It was nothing of the sort!

Let us examine the two Trigrams of this figure. The lower Trigram, number four (Earth), on one side means solidity and stability; on the other side, fixedness, constriction, and even restriction. When coupled with number one (Khien, or Lingam), we have on the bad side, constriction and restriction of the Great Khien energy and strength; on the good side, the solidity, stability, and consolidation of Earth, which is excellent for such things as concentration, making plans and decisions, and even for purposeful retirement from activity, though temporarily.

Earth represents form, and on one side we have the hampering or restriction in form. This is the point where that which has been solely activity must then be consolidated and stabilized in form. The Initiate in the Yi King should have no trouble in determining which is applicable.

In the man/woman relationship, the woman is too fixed, too stubborn; or there is conflict arising from being too docile and submissive. Can the man assert himself?

5 (10) LU

Water of Lingam

"Treading on the tiger's tail, yet it does not bite."

This means a person innocently protected, even from danger or stress. The text continues: "Those who tread the accustomed path and those who tread a level, easy path, who have due caution, and those who are resolute and those who examine the path beforehand—all these will not be harmed. The only one who will be harmed is the one who is a low man, but through bravado he treads defiantly a dangerous path."

Well! Bad fortune for him! Does the student need more proof than this that the texts are more often sermons—even sophistry—than realistic interpretations of each Hexagram?

Let us interpret this: The Trigram of Water means "pleased satisfaction"—complacence. Yes, there is the great energy, strength, and authority of Khien—whether representing superior people, superior conditions or strength, or the Great One, i.e., one's Divine Genius— the *real* Ruler. In any of these, the person is under a conditioned temporary benediction, and this is the "pleased satisfaction." In man/woman relationships it is excellent for the woman, though the man could deplete himself in granting the "benediction."

6 (6) SUNG

Moon of Lingam

"Contention" is the keyword of this Hexagram. Contention refers more to strong, active striving, but in combination with the Moon it is likely to *bring* contention unless there is self-restraint, good judgment, sincerity, and self-honesty. Many things ruled by these two Trigrams are incompatible in principle.

To explain this: The lower Trigram of Moon is well described as having more ambition than good judgment, and the project in question may be too big or incompatible. Remember that this Trigram also means "peril." The Moon Trigram describes adventurous or contentious persons or conditions.

It is better not to perpetuate contention but to be firm and correct. Do not advance or retreat, but stand firm. Be careful that you are not unequal to the contention. One may fully contend if one has invoked the wisdom, strength, and blessing of the Divine Genius. This Hexagram does indicate it to be "advantageous to see the Great Man"—whether literally or metaphorically.

Although this Hexagram advises restraint and caution, it can be a favorable figure if one conforms to its requirements—which is to invoke strength, wisdom, and support of the superior rather than to evoke one's own restricted or limited resources.

In a man/woman relationship it can be very good only if the woman remains completely invoking and quells the tendency to be active instead of passive, i.e., not evoking from one's self.

7 (25) WU WANG

Fire of Lingam

"Freedom from insincerity."

It means nothing of the sort! It is just good advice to use as an antidote against the great energy of this Hexagram.

The Trigram of Fire, with its Yang line at the bottom, is the first move out of Khwan, or Yoni. It spells thunder and lightning—sudden, great Fire energy. When this is coupled with Khien, the great initiating energy and force, it is like setting off a charge of dynamite. If done under intelligent and purposeful direction, its force is great and correct; but without intelligent direction and rectitude, this dynamite can have the same destructive effect as the force of this

Hexagram indicates to be possible.

If (we say "if") one is free from insincerity, then there will be progress and success, as the text states. By this word "sincerity" (which is so ubiquitous in the texts!) we are forced to conclude that it means self-honesty with good purpose and rectitude. In summation, it is a Hexagram of good auspice, of great moving energy and force, if the subject is sincere.

Due to the domination of Khien, there is no small assurance that all will go well or as just a matter of assured good fortune. I do not consider it good policy to defy or challenge the gods—or to ignore them.

In a man/woman relationship it emphasizes two extremes—either very favorable or very unfavorable.

8 (12) PHI

Khwan of Khien or Yoni of Lingam

"The big gone, the little come."

This deduction is based on the irrational idea that this Hexagram means midwinter. This cannot possibly be so with the Trigram of Khien dominating the Hexagram. Without pressing the point, it is sufficient to say that the Wans got themselves badly entrapped with this premise.

This Hexagram and its opposite, number 57, are distinctly unique (refer to number 57). If one has a question that involves another person besides him/herself, it is extremely important to make a coherent decision as to which Trigram, the upper or lower, fits the questioner and which one fits the other person. If it be a project, does it belong to the upper Trigram or to the lower Trigram?

In some cases it is easy to decide this. For example, if it is between man and woman, the lower Trigram is the woman. If the project is completely materialistic in quality, then the lower Trigram is considered. There are other projects that would be better attributed to the upper Trigram.

Usually the lower Trigram is completely receptive and cooperative with Khien, but we also have the strong emotions in Khwan, which can be very demanding. In this Hexagram there is a fine relationship between man and woman, but only under the condition that the woman's emotions and desires are not too demanding.

The lower Trigram is very good for that which has been started to be nourished and developed. It is an excellent figure for invoking the Great One, or invoking the help and wisdom of the Great One, though the text does not directly state this.

9 (9) HSIAO CHU

Lingam of Air

"Small restraint."

This is the name given by the text. This is due to the upper Trigram of Air meaning "easily penetrating" and the lower, the energetic Khien, brooks no restraint. We therefore have strength and energy coupled with flexibility. It is clear that there is no strong obstruction in pursuing one's objective. Air is the mental image of Khien—the Will—and obviously this applies to the first stages of a material project that will be easily carried out without serious obstruction.

The auspice is "progress, success, and good fortune," but it generally applies to the first stages rather than to the full development. Preliminary action can be very important, and this is the advice given in the Hexagram.

The upper Trigram represents the Great One which, in this case, puts small restraint upon the person or things belonging to the lower Trigram. This could even describe getting the best of one's superior, but note: this is no guarantee that it is essentially "good." We can say that self-honesty is in order, lest one be badly influenced by attaining success in small, menial things.

This is an excellent Hexagram for teaching others or for converting others to better aspirations. It is also good for receiving inspiration.

Generally mute on the subject of sex, the text states: "If the wife exercises restraint, no matter how correct, she is in a position of the man prosecuting his measures."

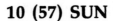

10 (57) SUN

Air of Air

"Under the conditions which it denotes,
there will be some little attainment and progress."

True, in material projects nothing big is indicated,
but for writing or for influencing others, this is a fine
augury.

We have the keywords: flexibility (allied to docili-
ty) and penetrating easy movement without restraint,
which allows for some little attainment, or moderate
achievement. Do not overlook the fact that this Hexagram is the very picture of the unstable. It is an instability that advises vigilance and correctness. Also
let the subject be well aware of the fact that while he or
she can make "easy penetration," he/she is also vul-

nerable to *being* penetrated. Both Trigrams are identical in this figure!

Heed also, that this is the flexibility of the mind itself. It is also the "line of least resistance" urge!

The text well describes the rattlebrain type of mind who "hides his head and employs diviners and exorcists in a way bordering on confusion," then continues with the typical ridiculous inconsistency that "there will be good fortune and no error." With considerable more sense, the text further states, "If the man has lost the axe with which he executed his decisions, no matter how firm he be, there will be evil."

In a man/woman relationship it is required that they mutually make good decisions and that they do not lose their axes!

11 (37) KIA ZHAN

Sun of Air

In the text this Hexagram means a household or family, and the proper regulation of the household is the employed symbolism. All this is a *deus ex machina* symbolism. What follows is merely preaching and sophistry.

In looking to the two Trigrams for meaning, we observe Trigram number three, the Sun, brilliant realization, under Trigram number two, Air, which is the mental concept.

Note that the lower Trigram, Sun, describes one of a well-integrated personality (brilliant realization). This person has free course because of the upper Trigram being Air. The Daemon, Genius, Id, Great One does not assume the part of Jehovah in warrior mood—ruthless and despotic—rather he is tolerant and agreeable with his partner. The same applies to the conditions of the project in question, if any. The text is wrong in stating the necessity of "restrictive regulations" and "stern severity." If the person be the negative aspect of Sun—the big-shot or megalomaniac— stern severity would be futile anyway!

The text does not so state, but it is good advice for the subject to look to the Great One and also to invoke wisdom instead of wholly relying upon one's intelligence and reasoning mind.

In man/woman relationships, the Sun describes a woman who is inclined to be dominant, forceful, and masculine, yet it describes her as a fully integrated Woman (with a capital W) with great understanding and capabilities. Fortunate indeed would be the man who meets this latter type—particularly if he be the one described in the upper Trigram.

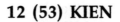

12 (53) KIEN

Earth of Air

"Gradually advancing."

The text preaches a long sermon on just how one should gradually advance. This is worthless to explain the Hexagram. Essentially, the Hexagram does not mean "gradually advancing" except in the sense that everything in the universe is advancing!

In quoting from my book *The Incredible I Ching* I have stated: "The lower Trigram, Earth, the body or the set physical pattern, regulates or binds the Trigram of Air, the mind or mental image. In other words, it is good for maintaining anything in a stable way in conformity with certain fixed patterns or conditions."

This means to make something solid, stable, and

consolidated out of something that has the intangible or insubstantial quality of air—on whatever plane it may manifest—and bringing one's ideas down to Earth. On the negative side there can be too much fixedness and constriction. At times and under some conditions, the text's admonition can be well taken, i.e., to bring about this consolidation "by gradual, successive steps," but this is not the meaning of the figure.

This is an excellent Hexagram for concentration. It indicates fixation of the mind—it is not rambling or flighty.

This is a Hexagram that represents much inflexibility: stern, hard, fixed laws and customs that do not bend according to the circumstances. Unbending, unyielding, dogmatic. The solidity of Earth is at the crossroads—useful versus constrictive.

In man/woman relationships it is very good when coupled with fixed ideals versus restrictive chores.

13 (61) KUNG FU

Water of Air

"Inmost sincerity."

This is merely good advice; it is not the meaning of the figure. The text rightly states: "We have the attributes of pleased satisfaction (Water) and flexible penetration (Air). Sincerity is thus symbolized." This is just fancy. Actually "sincerity," or self-honesty, is a requirement in order to get the best from any Hexagram.

The upper Trigram of Air represents "superiors," or high conditions, which can both easily penetrate and be penetrated. It is therefore condescending and easygoing in relation to those of the lower Trigram, Water. There is no contention or dissatisfaction between the upper and lower Trigrams. There is much mutual response leading to satisfaction.

This Hexagram describes the easy and happy union of the mind with the exalted imagination. It well describes fiction, poetry, music, and drama of a pleasant, imaginative type and the type of person relating to these arts. The vulnerable side is the overemphasis of pleasure and imagination, which could even border on the psychopathic. It is well to note that there is the possibility of a lack of stability in this combination of Air and Water; hence the injunction of the text to be of "inmost sincerity." It is encouraging to note that, in welcoming inspiration, the upper Trigram transforms that which is below. It is a good auspice for "crossing the Great Stream."

In man/woman relationships, it is one of the very best Hexagrams, particularly in sincerely desiring inspiration.

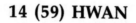

14 (59) HWAN

Moon of Air

"Dissipation or dispersion."

This is a good description. It corresponds with the lower Trigram of Moon, and it has full course under Air. But then Wan's son, writing after the manner of diviners, proceeds blithely to state good auspice for all six lines! His philosophy: "There is a scattering of what should be scattered, and what should not be scattered may be collected." All this is very well, but it is not very realistic nor is it practical. It is practical only for the truly Great One to play both Tao and Jehovah.

To make anything good out of this Hexagram, the text enjoins one to "retire to the Ancestral Temple"— to invoke the aid of the spirits, and secondly, to enlist the help of other good, capable people. One should also muster all of his (or her) "contrivances" (for security), and "discarding any regard to his own person," cross the Great Stream—to venture beyond the scope of this Hexagram. All to be done with what is right, firm, and correct.

Every Hexagram has some good augury, and for whatever needs to be dissipated, dispersed, scattered, and alienated because of its own bad qualities, this is the Hexagram for it. This figure is Moon—restriction—of Air, the mind. This can be used for good, but it is more apt to spell immaturity, incapability, overambition, or a scattering of forces by untamed emotions and strivings.

In summation, it is a bad augury concerning the level of the average person. It is of good use only to the superior individual. This also applies to the man/woman relationship.

15 (42) YI

Fire of Air

"Adding or increasing."

This name is derived by a quaint contrivance: "The upper Trigram is diminished and the lower added to"!

The lower Trigram is Fire—great energy, which is given free course by the upper Trigram of Air. This also means the energy and force of the mind is given to the mental concept. A better name for this Hexagram would be "Unrestricted energy of Fire." This is good, but it can also be bad when this fiery energy and drive is not under intelligent control and direction.

Note that all three lines of the upper Trigram are of opposite polarity to the corresponding three lines of the lower Trigram. This means complete response between the two on all three planes. This is a most powerful Hexagram. The lower Trigram is a great driving energy of the body, the emotions, and the instincts. It is given full response from the upper Trigram—there is nothing saying "no" from above unless it be one's inherent superiority and wisdom. The text states: "There will be advantage in every movement which shall be undertaken, even to crossing the Great Stream." If this be taken as a good augury, it is "advantageous" to carry out some act of "violence"—at least let one not get into the habit of being "restricted" when the Hexagram is not of such "advantageous" augury.

In man/woman relationships one can see the very good and the very bad aspects, ultimately, regardless of the temporary.

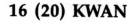

16 (20) KWAN

Yoni of Air

The text describes this Hexagram as "Showing, manifesting"—also "contemplating, looking at." The reason being that it "shows how the upper (Air) manifests to the lower (Yoni) and the lower contemplates the higher." This hits the mark to some extent, even though it is Yoni that "manifests" instead of Air. Also Yoni *invokes* the upper, rather than "contemplating" it. It is tiresome to contradict the text, but again let us examine the meaning of the figure by its component Trigrams: nourishment, reception, expansion and development of the mental concept or mind. We may also correctly say that the lower Trigram, Yoni, invokes and *manifests* the higher. One wonders why the text does not advise: "It is well to see the Great One." Yoni, being the lower Trigram, is Woman—at least from the Chinese point of view. Should not the woman look up to her husband?

For example: Khwan, the woman, supports the initiatory activity. She nourishes and develops it into manifestation—the child. This is a good illustration of this Hexagram. The upper Trigram, Air, is the initial force of the mental concept—the plan—easily penetrating and easily penetrated. Thus the Hexagram represents the *development* of something that has not yet been fully developed. It is the feminine nourishment and development of a larger manifestation, or something more concrete. The vulnerable side of this figure is in giving full course to the desires and emotions, which are excessive and without restraint.

In the man/woman relationship it is particularly good for the woman.

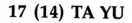

17 (14) TA YU

Lingam of Sun

The text names this Hexagram "Great Havings," or an abundance of the good. "There will be great progress and success. The threatening danger is the pride which it is likely to engender."

The Trigram Lingam, the great creative energy, is acting upon the Sun—realization and the realized Self. Line number five is the Superior One. There is a reciprocal sincerity between this and all other line positions. He is tolerant (even the Daemon), but there is an inherent proper majesty.

This Hexagram means the brilliant realization of the creative impulse—Lingam to Sun. It indicates a current condition of "great havings" but no auspice for further acquisition—just brilliance in the present state of "having." This Hexagram also indicates "brilliant intelligence," even to the point of initiated wisdom.

Here is another good observation from the text: "The feudal prince presents his offering to the Son of Heaven. A small man would not be equal to this." This implies that a superior person should keep the use of his or her great resources under restraint and not be arrogant. "If the strength is tempered, then Heaven gives its approval."

While no further greater accumulation is promised in this figure, it is a most auspicious time to put everything in good order—to consolidate one's "havings." Ultimately, this may assure greater accumulation in the future.

In man/woman relationships, both Trigrams are essentially masculine. It would be a rare and great woman to fit this.

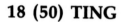

18 (50) TING

Air of Sun

"The Cauldron."

For the most part, the text treats the cauldron as a symbol of nourishment, whether it is for cooking food as nourishment or for the nourishment of talent and virtue. "There is no changer of the character equal to the furnace and cauldron."

This Hexagram is *the* Great Transformer. King Wan's son sees the person much distressed because of the transformations upon the person. But this is for the person's own good—his or her self-created necessity. The writer seems to be well aware of this because, contrary to the general rule of seeing a rather negative condition in the end (the sixth line), he says of this line position: "The cauldron has rings of jade—great good fortune. All action in every way is advantageous." It would have been better to say that the subject is brought to a realization of his or her own brilliant higher self.

I would go further than calling it the Great Transformer. Ting is *the* Hexagram of *transmutation*. This is the Great Transmutation in the high magick of the Eucharist. This is the transmutation accomplished in high sex magick.

Under the auspice of this figure there comes the transformation aspired to, in its end result. But let not the subject suppose that his or her unworthiness will pass without challenge. His attendant faults or insincerity will also meet with transformation—to the subject's discomfort, perhaps.

In man/woman relationships there is none better for sex magick.

19 (30) LI

Sun of Sun

"Brilliance, intelligence."

This Hexagram is a double Sun. The text also states that it is "inhering to, or adhering to." This is correct. The two Yin lines picture the Ruler—both the ordinary person and the superior person—as being fully receptive and cooperative to the strength of the lower line as well as to the wisdom of the upper line. This understanding is due to the reception of wisdom, which implies "intelligence" and realization.

On the vulnerable side of this figure, the subject acts "coarsely and vehemently, and with inordinate pride." The stronger indication of it is "Adherence to the right in reverence towards his (or her) self-realization." All this is the distinction between the low person and the one who is sincere and adheres to the correct with humility. Remember that in every Hexagram there is the unregenerate person and the regenerate person. This also applies to the conditions pertaining to a question.

Since there are no responding lines in this figure, the two Trigrams being identical in quality, there is a demand that the subject adhere to the best in the figure. The same principle applies to the subject's affairs; then there will be free course and brilliant success.

The advice is to invoke the good strength of the lower line and the unseen higher strength and wisdom of the upper line.

In the man/woman relationship, the good force of this Hexagram is entirely of the invoking, and none of the evoking.

20 (56) LU

Earth of Sun

"Strangers: travelling abroad."

This description is justifiable only in the sense that the lower Trigram (Earth) applies to low people among high people (Sun), the entrenched inhabitants.

The fixed Earth is the restricted image of Sun, the realized self, or conditions. The better side is "consolidation" of what is realized. This is based upon the assumption that nothing is completed to its ultimate or is forever stable; hence it is advised to take advantage of the consolidation principle of this Hexagram.

Advancement is not promised except in a small way, but consolidation prepares for future advance. On the one side is a stubbornness and unjustifiable pride (Sun); on the other side is a firm, stable condition which contains neither need nor ambition to advance (Earth). Materialistic, fixed stability versus constricted ideals. Low men and good drives are restricted, and the upper Trigram (supposedly superiors) is in the same position, although of better status.

Probably the best advice is to let go of the fixed idea of being self-sufficient and to seek help and support. This is not good for rivalry or contention.

Man/woman relationships are not auspicious unless the woman seeks to give solid support to the highest qualities of the man and can give up her materialistic desires—then very good.

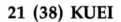

21 (38) KUEI

Water of Sun

"Disunion, division."
"There is diversity, even though in general agreement."

After opening with these gloomy notions, the text proceeds blithely and inconsistently to assert good auspice for all six line positions. It is sophistically explained that the "fire of Sun goes upwards and the water of the lake flows downward," hence "division, disunion, and alienation."

Number five Water (pleased satisfaction) of number three Sun (the realized self or brilliant realization). Here we may see so much self-satisfaction that one has no yen for real friendship nor deigns to ask for help or cooperation; but this, in itself, does not spell disunion and mutual alienation—it would merely be the result of the "low side" of the Hexagram. On the other side of the Hexagram is the humble pleased satisfaction in attaining some realization or "brilliance." Naturally, low people fall into the state of egotistical self-satisfaction. The Hexagram indicates "resting on the oars," and the result will be as the text states: "success in small matters."

There is very good response between lines two and three and lines five and six. If the aim is sincerely high, it is auspicious to both invoke and evoke the "genial rain of Heaven"—the happy union of the Yang and Yin in Nature; therefore, it is excellent for man/woman relationships.

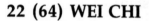

22 (64) WEI CHI

Moon of Sun

"Struggle for completion."

In the philosophy of the Yi, with its ever-changing polarity and position, "completion" is never accomplished (i.e., there is no perfect and abiding state).

The metaphor used in the text is, "A young fox gets its tail wet in trying to cross the stream." This aptly describes immaturity (or inability), with the attendant condition of more ambition than good judgment—aims, plans, or drives beyond one's presently existing ability or present scope of development. It is a good metaphor.

This Hexagram has both a good and a bad auspice. The auspice of the three top lines (three grades of superiors) is good, but only under the following restrictive conditions: (1) that the person (or project) not be overambitious and adventuresome; (2) that there be intelligent restraint and recognition of the involved difficulties; (3) that there be due preparation before invading the Demon region; (4) that one have the bright intelligence, moral force, and sincerity of a "superior" man; and (5) to remain quiet, at the proper times, in the confidence of his or her own power and not try to prove him/herself by contending with peril. Seems contradictory? Yes! It is a perilous Hexagram, and there is a thin line between success and failure.

Man/woman relationships: like all of the foregoing.

23 (21) SHIH HO

Fire of Sun

"Union by gnawing."

This is a handy phrase but not relevant. Fire, number seven, is exciting action and energy of a willful nature and is in conjunction with Sun, number three, intelligence and realization. There is only small agreement between these two Trigrams. There is excessive energy that is not intelligently directed, and that lacks diligent action and discipline.

Then what can be done to achieve successful progress? (1) Start nothing that is not intelligently planned; (2) exert diligent action under self-discipline; (3) avoid instinctive and emotional action; and (4) exercise strong force and energy to remove obstacles.

The entire problem of this Hexagram is that obstacles must be revamped or bested before there can be good cooperation.

The next step then is for the person to decide whether he or she or the project in question is capable of overcoming any blind, sudden, emotional drive for forceful action, because from the fire and energy of the lower Trigram emanates an emotional and almost automatic drive for forceful action without capable and intelligent direction. Generally, the result of the activity must await a future time for its material support and full development.

Man/woman relationships are not auspicious, except under good direction in the great, exciting energy and drive for self-realization.

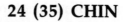

24 (35) CHIN

Khwan of Sun

"To advance."

All good people (and things) advance unless close to termination, so this is not a very specific name. "Great development and increase (lower Trigram Khwan) of brilliant realization (upper Trigram Sun)" better describes this Hexagram.

The lower Trigram symbolizes the materialistic and the desires wanting to be filled up. This indicates some preliminary difficulties, but not persisting long.

The lower Trigram is "invoking," and the upper is "evoking." Therefore, the "superior" is successful in evoking the good support and cooperation of the "inferior." The sole adverse phase of the Hexagram is if the upper becomes enchanted with the drive of the lower to be "filled up" and the brilliance of the upper abandons itself—but this would be only temporary and the "advance and increase" in growth and development is assured, ultimately. "Great Increase" describes this Hexagram better than "Advancing"—increase in realization and brilliant manifestation.

Let the superior not be hard on the strong desires or rebelliousness of the lower; rather, let the intelligence of the upper combine with the support of the lower—as if by magick.

Man/woman relationships: none better. Great for the woman, and by reflex response, equally great for the man.

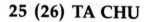

25 (26) TA CHU

Khien of Earth

The text names this Hexagram "The Great Accumulation," which is an excellent name. The text also well states, "advantageous to cross the great stream."

Number one Khien is great energy and strength; however, it is under the dominion of the upper, number four, which is "fixed" and therefore works a restraint upon the exercise of forceful energy. That which is repressed results in an accumulated strength and volume, especially of "virtue." Certainly this is so if the energy is controlled with intelligence and purpose. However, psychologists know the negative side of this thing called repression. Is there much of this condition of repression in this case? Only with low inferiors who lack virtue and intelligent, willed self-direction.

Although there are some unfavorable indications, we should note that the urge to accumulate by the exercise of restraint comes from the upper Trigram position—not the lower—and it is therefore of good result, mostly. Compare this Hexagram with Hexagram number four, where the Trigrams are the same but in reversed position.

This Hexagram is excellent for intelligently consolidating one's strength for the future. Man/woman relationships: Indicates the woman to be acting in a very assertive manner, which could be good only if the man is in a state of great receptivity.

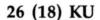

26 (18) KU

Air of Earth

"Painful services to perform."

The text blithely states, "Great progress and success to him who deals properly with the condition represented by this Hexagram." But who would "deal properly," i.e., perform painful services both efficiently and willingly, without complaining? Obviously, a person of high virtue with a sense of responsibility.

What do the two Trigrams really spell? Number two Air, the mind, under number four Earth, binding restriction: At best, the enforced solution of material things. The nature of the Trigram Air is "easy penetration or easily penetrated," but here the "penetration" seems to be limited to some sort of demand or compulsion to be concerned only with small materialistic affairs, although with some due credit and reward.

This Hexagram is good for concentration and for any mental work that requires single-mindedness; but, again, this is generally considered to be "painful" by lazy, indifferent people.

The text states that there will be advantage *in trying* to cross the great stream—this is trying to advance beyond the sphere of rather fixed limitations. Even though not completely successful, it is advantageous.

The highest indicated augury of this Hexagram is that the "superior" is receptive to the high aspiration of the "inferior," and therefore one should serve only one's Higher Self—the real superior.

Man/woman relationships: It is advised to limit the relation to bring about a restoration of soundness and vigor.

27 (22) PI

Sun of Earth

The text names this Hexagram "Ornament—Adorning." It continues with "There should be free course (only in what the Hexagram denotes) and only small advantage in advancing."

Number three Sun, brilliance and intelligence, is limited in scope by the lower position, number four Earth, limiting fixation. Yet there is "free course" in Sun to express its inherent brilliance by "ornament and adorning," thus making the best of the limitation. The superior one, however, resorts to personal adornment only by dressing in a "white robe and is satisfied to see beautiful "ornament" in nature and in his environment.

Due to the limitations of this Hexagram, the best

advised procedure is to undertake *preparation*. In this limited advancing condition, it is well to note that "proper" ornament leads to transformation. This is a psychological principle well known in ritualistic magick. Occultly considered, Sun is the realization of Earth, the physical body. But Earth is the upper Trigram, and hence the urge to idealize it in some manner—by following the simple urge for beautiful customs and ethics—ameliorating ornament and brilliance.

This Hexagram, therefore, rather than indicating advancing activity, indicates a time for preparing by "adornment," or beautiful plans and preparation. The beautiful marriage ceremony is an expression of this Hexagram.

Man/woman relationships: as indicated in the foregoing.

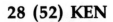

28 (52) KEN

Earth of Earth

"Resting and arresting."

The text well observes that any attempt to advance will be in error. Only the superior man or woman has good fortune if he or she rests in principle and is not motivated into action by selfish thoughts and external events or people.

This is one of the eight Hexagrams in which the upper and lower Trigrams are identical. Such Hexagrams are almost of an abstract nature. It is difficult to envision, in this case, the principles of Trigram Earth—fixed, constricted immobility—operating entirely and exclusively within its own sphere. The immobility of the mountain is immobile to anything else.

Suffice it to say that, for all practical purposes and considerations, the force of "resting and arresting" is strong enough so that it is almost futile to combat or circumvent the condition. In this respect, King Wan's son contradicts himself in describing the third line position as "The loins need to be controlled (kept at rest) because the heart glows with suppressed excitement. Consequently the situation is perilous." He either had a continual ache of the testicles or could not suppress his style of writing after the manner of the diviners!

This Hexagram is good for absolute body rest.

In man/woman relationships, the foregoing is indicative.

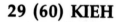

29 (60) KIEH

Water of Earth

The text states that this means "diminishing or diminution" of what is unduly excessive. This is not very well named. Earth is a limitation or fixing of any Water, or excessive desire for pleasure or satisfaction. The keyword "diminishing" tends to lead one astray.

Water, being in the lower Trigram position, could indicate a very strong desire for pleasure and satisfaction among the low, inferior people, but the influence of the upper Trigram (whether it refers to conditions or superior people) causes some restraining influence. This should probably be called the ideal situation. However, there is some conflict between the desires of the lower and the austerity of the upper, which should not be completely ignored.

The text states that there will be "good fortune," "freedom from error and advantage in every movement"—but only if he or she is unselfish, generous, and restrains his/her wrath and desires. This may seem to be an excessive "if," but we should note that the nature of the Hexagram is in conformity with the "if." The Hexagram indicates stable, pleased satisfaction, steady-flowing and not excessive.

Note that the polarity (Yang and Yin) of the corresponding lines of both Trigrams are mutually different. This indicates strong and good mutual response between the two Trigrams and very little conflict.

In man/woman relationships it is good for sex magick, as indicated by line number six. Increase not subject to diminution. Fixation of pleasurable desires in matter or the body.

30 (4) MENG

Moon of Earth

The text describes this as "Youthful inexperience" and continues, "In the case which it presupposes, there will be progress and success."

What this progress may be is not stated, nor can I define it. The upper (superior) Trigram is Earth, which is solid, fixed, consolidating, and in its best implication, practicality. If one of "inability" (referring to the lower Trigram of Moon) is forced to become practical, and tackles only what is consistent with the ability or opportunity, then there could be progress and success. Example: A certain well-known orchestra leader had first tried to be an accordion player, but he did not have the ability, nor could he write good orchestral arrangements. He hired an arranger and an outstanding accordion player and has since become a very successful orchestra leader.

This indicates that one can, and should, recognize an inadequate condition. Yet, by resourceful practicality he can attain progress and success. The text stresses "sincerity." This implies self-appraisal and self-honesty in considering any course.

It is advisable not to have more ambition than good judgment. Neither envision nor tackle projects that, in being sincere, honest and practical, you should suspect are beyond your known ability. This does not mean that one should not have the idea of the project in its essential nature.

A man/woman relationship is good only for the woman.

32 (23) PO

Yoni of Earth

"Falling. Overthrowing."

This name could be correct only if the text is correct in stating that this Hexagram belongs to the ninth month, which is not correct.

The lower Trigram indicates "inferior" people, or the masses. Yoni being in this position indicates many and strong desires yearning to be satisfied or filled up. The upper Trigram of Earth does not indicate much that is satisfying to the desires. However, we may say that it is good that inordinate desires do not meet with anything other than solidity and immobility.

On the other side, solidity and stability being the upper position represents something very good under the conditions of this Hexagram, and the lower Trigram nourishes and supports the stability of superior people and projects.

There are inordinate demands of inferiors and desires, while at the same time, the lower gives nourishment and support toward stability.

No actual movement in any direction is of much value. It may even be difficult. It is better described as a preparation for advance or movement, rather than movement in itself. It is only ultimately, as indicated by line six, that anything or anyone acquires fresh vigor for advance. Usually, the top line does not refer to a person. It refers to the invisible "ruler," one's own Daemon, or the invisible results of one's past actions.

In man/woman relationships it is not very propitious.

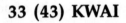

33 (43) KWAI

Lingam of Water

"Displacing or removing."

It is good advice to be prepared to displace or remove some possible challenging people or things, but this does not make it the meaning of the Hexagram.

The "superior" is the upper Trigram of Water, which is self-complacency and in some cases, indulgence in pleased satisfaction, while the "inferior" Trigram is great strength, energy, and demanding drive. This is very good for the inferior dealing with a superior, if the inferior is sincere and correct and does not go too far in challenging the superior.

The upper Trigram represents one's Daemon, the

hidden director, the higher phases of the mind. It is a type of temporary karma, and in this case, because the Trigram is Water, there is a complacency and pleased satisfaction that allows one to fully proceed according to one's own conscious force, energy, and initiative. Yet strangely enough, if one is not sincere and correct, the whole thing degenerates into an excessive offensive against one's superior self, which will certainly boomerang back.

This can be a very good Hexagram for energetically starting something with the confidence that good fortune is promised. But the good fortune itself should be regarded as something only loaned to one and to be gratefully received. Do not tempt the gods!

In man/woman relationships, it is not to be recommended. Feminine aggressiveness versus an easygoing or complacent man, which will surely run its course into displacing.

34 (28) TA KWO

Air of Water

"A weak beam."

This is a fair name under the concept of being a bridge that can carry success only in small proportions. In fact, there is indicated easy attainment of success in a small way, but not on a grand scale.

This figure, being composed of the Trigrams of Air and Water, indicates that there is an easygoing, superficial satisfaction, but it is lacking substance. The text symbolizes this as "an old man with a young wife and an old woman with a young husband"—an easy attainment to pleased satisfaction of the desires!

Air is the mental concept of Water, which is pleased satisfaction easily attained. But it is not of substantial duration. Water, as the "superior," indicates pleased satisfaction and complacence. Air, as the "inferior," indicates a mercurial cleverness and exigent adaptability. If the inferior is sincere, there is a good relationship with the superior. Otherwise, there may be an attempt to take advantage of the superior.

There are little or no demands upon the questioner. And there is free course for diversions, amusements, vacations, and all mental occupations that are not too weighty. It is a good augury to deal in a pleasant way with people.

Line five, the "King," "may not carry out the requirements of the times, even though able to do so." This is correct.

Man/woman relationships: superficially good, but note the above indications.

35 (49) KO

Sun of Water

"Changing. Advantage comes from being firm and correct and then there is great progress and success."

The text states that the "change" is believed in only after it has been accomplished! This may be intended to indicate that the changing is the end result of the auspice of the Hexagram, rather than its actual meaning.

The text goes on to preach that change is received by the multitudes with dislike and only fairly received when proven necessary. This may be good preaching, but the Hexagram means something quite different. The lower Trigram, number three, Sun, is a superior Trigram held by the inferior position. It is the intel-

ligence and brilliance of the inferior that would be
initiating the change.

> Proceed not hastily, time's a friend to thee.
> Haste may wreck all; discuss thy plans untried.
> First gain men's confidence, then saddle and ride.
> Swift as a tiger—with the Yi for guide.
> Confirm thy change with firm sincerity.
>
> Fom the G∴B∴G∴ interpretation

Sun (realization) of Water—pleasure brings about
a realization of the imperfection of images and a reconciliation to transforming change.

This is a good augury, both for dealing with common people (if correctly) and with the "superior." It is
good for projects that are not too ambitious or on too
large a scale.

Man/woman relationships: good for higher transformation if under due preparation and not carried out
too hastily.

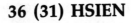

36 (31) HSIEN

Earth of Water

"Mutually influencing, all together, jointly."

This meaning is evidently arrived at by the corresponding lines of the two Trigrams being of opposite or corresponding polarity. But there are 16 such Hexagrams! In all 64 Hexagrams there is one Trigram that "influences" the other Trigram!

Here we have the materialistic Earth operating under the complacent Water. The text states that "there will be free course and success" upon the fulfillment of the conditions implied. In all the Hexagrams King Wan states just what the conditions are to be fulfilled. Here are the conditions: Aim for stability and consolidation of one's affairs or of oneself under sincerity and correctness. This is the good side of Earth, but do not succumb to the other side of Earth, which is senseless fix-edness, stubbornness, or gross materialism. Water, holding the superior position, is complacently in accord.

This is a very good augury for consolidating one's efforts and affairs if one is not inordinately ambitious. There is free course, but this does not mean advantage in pushing forward. It promises good, consolidating security while temporarily resting in pleased satisfaction. Correct aims are surely effective in bringing about transformation.

In the man/woman relationship it is best to merely bring things to a firm foundation and to advance later. Ideally, this in itself can bring about a transformation.

37 (58) TUI

Water of Water

"Under the conditions of this Hexagram
there will be progress and attainment."

Both Trigrams are Water; therefore, the meaning
is "pleased satisfaction, pleasure and complacency."
The main conditions are firmness, correctness, and
sincerity, and they are not to be submerged in sensuous pleasure or lassitude.

> Appease thyself: harmonious in thy sphere.
> Single thy will, most utterly sincere.
> Turn NOT aside when siren pleasures woo:
> Search well thyself to make thy purpose clear.
> Too trustful customers may buy too dear.

'Tis pleasant to be captain of thy crew.
Still waters may run deep and free,
But mistake not slackness for philosophy.

From the G∴B∴G∴ interpretation

Even the superior one encourages conversation with all and the stimulus thus derived.

Both Trigrams are of the Yin nature and are capable of invoking and evoking attraction. This is the Hexagram of Attraction. But let there be no great attraction for wasteful, sensuous pleasure. Yet there is good course in seeking and following the path of pleasure when sparked with constructive purpose or ideals.

For any project, this Hexagram gives the necessary preliminary attractive activity, rather than any sustaining development. It has the principle of power to attract the multitudes, who are willing to give supporting energy, but they must be attracted to it.

In man/woman relationships it is very good, if carried out under the implied conditions contained in the above poetry.

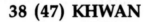

38 (47) KHWAN

Moon of Water

"Straightened or distressed."

The text has pictured the symbolism of a tree, among larger trees, which does not have sufficient room to spread its branches. Therefore, the name. This is indeed an unfavorable augury.

The very best Hexagrams contain some unfavorable implications, and in the same manner, we may see some good in the worst Hexagrams, such as this one. The text continues: "Even though the augury is very distressing, there still may be some progress and success for the *really* great man, if he be firm and correct."

How many people are "really great men"? Let us

be realistic. Yet one might emulate what this great one would do under the "straightened" circumstances. Under the conditions of this figure, the superior person would not allow the feeling of being "distressed," but would play the part of the upper Trigram, Water, and maintain an unruffled feeling, content in the faith that the bad cycle will pass.

It is good advice that one does not enter into any project that is under this bad augury. Wait! Growth and development can take place even with the "straightened tree." Perchance it is better to follow a different project.

Take note that the "straightened and distressed" comes from the lower Trigram, not the upper. It is a good time to seek the guidance and wisdom of the Great One.

Man/woman relationships: no!

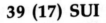

39 (17) SUI

Fire of Water

"Adherents. Following after. Seeking: Obeisance."

This is the ideal to be strived for rather than the direct implications of the Hexagram. Ideally, there is a cooperation and reconciliation between the upper Trigram of Water, which is easy complacency, and the lower Trigram of Fire, which is strong, exciting energy. Thus, the superior person welcomes adherents who loyally strive for harmony and satisfaction.

Naturally, there is the other side, where uncontrolled fiery energy challenges the status of pleased satisfaction. But being forewarned, the person of sincerity and integrity can forestall this. Then the drive for a harmonious pleased satisfaction takes the ascendancy.

144

Wit of age employ,
Make sure thy way is straight.
Follow excellence with eager gait.
The King may sacrifice with joy.

The G∴B∴G∴ interpretation

Ideally, the fiery will cooperating with pleasure. The ordinary person (lower Trigram) is driven by energetic will and is not hampered or denied by the superior Trigram of the agreeable Water. This is a free course to energetic activity and progress, and success is indicated. But not in great things—not a great project—though it is a good augury for satisfaction.

Man/woman relationships: For good results, the position of the two Trigrams should be reversed, unless it be a masculine woman and a feminine man. However, the man might gain an adherent even in a highly energetic woman if he is a superior man.

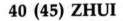

40 (45) ZHUI

Yoni of Water

"Collected together, things collected: union."

This is well named, though it also implies full development. Yoni is great capacity and nourishment and development of a state of satisfaction, Water. There is no dispersion or separation for ill. Thus, "collecting" instead of disunion. There is union between the high and the low. The desires of the "inferiors" are in accord with the acquiescence of the "superior," be it one's own desires or those of others.

The augury indicates development and completion to a state of high satisfaction. It is even pleasing to the Great One, and therefore well to "repair to the Ancestral Temple and meet the Great Man."

This is the full expansion of satisfaction, or pleasure. The other side of this figure is uncontrolled avid desires for pleasure, and it is well to keep things within their due bounds and to be prepared for unforeseen contingencies that result from such inordinate desires. Excellent though this Hexagram be, it is well to remember that there is an adverse side to every Hexagram.

Man/woman relationships: In that operation known as high sex magick, this is one of the best Hexagrams. But note well all of the above conditions, as one must do with all Hexagrams.

41 (5) HSU

Lingam of Moon

"Waiting."

This is not the real implication of the figure; it is merely advice. It is not even good advice except for the superior man, for a superior project, or for one who has the necessary wisdom and intuition that is required under these conditions. In fact, the "inferiors"—on all planes—are very strong, even correct, and instead of waiting, it is good to challenge the incapacity of the superior position. A weak ruler and his henchmen are vulnerable to the challenging strength and activity of the lower Trigram, Lingam.

The text states that this is "strength confronted by peril," but fails to note that it also is peril and ineptness confronted by strength.

The superior is in a restricted and vulnerable position. He cannot expect to have good followers because Lingam does not "follow." Rather than having docile followers, he must have followers who take strong, responsible positions, as denoted by the lower Trigram. Let the superior call to his aid his material resources and the activity of his physical vehicles (followers), even though they may be devoid of inspiration, wisdom, and intuition but are correct in strength and activity. It is not the time for progress and advancement, therefore the advice of waiting. Sincerity, firmness, and correctness are very essential; otherwise there will be peril and restriction.

In man/woman relationships it is unfavorable. There is no inspiration, aspiration, or idealism in this Hexagram, and it tends to be combative.

42 (48) ZING

Air of Moon

The text names this "The Well," saying that even though the town declines, the pure water of the central community well remains as a source of supply. This is merely optimistic preaching. No matter how bad the situation, do not be disheartened. There is always the source of the Spirit. But this does not describe the Hexagram!

This is the mental concept of Air—of the restricted Moon—the universe, or Self. The best thing that the superior person can do is to resort to the rational and logical intellect to understand the deficiencies in any project and in one's self, which should lead to self-cultivation; thereby he or she may stimulate mutual helpfulness between him/herself and others. This also applies to inferiors. Here, then, can be the "common well," or fountain, of supply and increase.

We may say that the only good augury of this Hexagram is the ability to use the rational intellect, thereby coming to an understanding of all the deficiencies, restrictions, and difficulties—all of which can lead to self-cultivation and improvement. This can lead to mutual helpfulness with others and with one's many and various propensities and forces.

There is nothing to indicate much progress and advancement in any materialistic project. There is only the correcting of faults and arriving at an understanding of the difficulties and restrictions.

In man/woman relationships it is superficial.

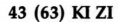

43 (63) KI ZI

Sun of Moon

"Past or the completed. Helping, completing."

It means nothing of the sort! King Wan used this Hexagram to picture the final overthrow of the tyrant king and the establishment of his own rulership. The description of the six line positions is even worse.

This is the realization (Sun) of the usually restrictive Moon in all things and people. It promises help to be attained and full success—but only in small things, due to the restrictive Moon. The Moon is incapable and perilous, but Sun ameliorates the condition enough to indicate some realization, though it is advised not to attempt anything new on a large scale.

The ideal polarity of the lines is that the bottom

line should be Yang, and then the polarity is alternated in each succeeding line. This is the only Hexagram that fills this condition. And to be consistent it should be the best of all other Hexagrams! But no Hexagram is of much good augury that has Moon for its upper Trigram! Actually, if these two Trigrams were reversed—which would be violating all line rules—it would be a better figure. In this Hexagram, the superior is "dim" and the inferior is "brilliant." It is good for inferiors outshining superiors. The physical vehicles and the intellectual mind is superior to what little exists in the superior Trigram.

In man/woman relationships it is not very good.

44 (39) KIEN

Earth of Moon

The text very well names this figure "Incompetence in the feet," meaning the inability to advance under the conditions of number four, Earth, which is fixedness. Moon is ineptness and inability or peril faced with the solidity and immobility of Earth.

Let us search for something favorable in this unfavorable figure. The superior subject and the conditions of any projects are in a state of peril and distress. What can be done in conformity with the nature of this figure? The answer is to work to consolidate and arrange all affairs (Earth) so that the peril and restriction of Moon can be balanced. It is possible to secure some help from solid, down-to-earth types of people. One must attain stability rather than have ideas of advancement. Let it be discreet, small movement alternating with discreet inactivity and consolidation.

> Adamant! Friends come to prosecute thy plan.
> Advance not! Wait for aid from the Great Man!

> From the G∴B∴G∴ interpretation

Esoterically, this Hexagram is the formulation in matter of restriction—the incarnation or sacrifice.

Under this Hexagram it is well and auspicious to examine one's self and to cultivate one's virtues. The fifth line represents the King, and this line is very well aspected. This favors both the exercise of aspiration and the receiving of inspiration.

In the man/woman relationship, it is solely under the conditions described above. There is no bright promise.

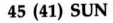

45 (41) SUN

Water of Moon

The text names this "Joints of bamboo," meaning regular divisions, such as the four divisions of the day and the year. But this implies the idea of "regulating and restraining," and it is only by this regulation that good results will be realized.

Let us first examine the unfavorable aspects of this figure. There can be an unregulated drive or desire for pleasure and satisfaction, of Water, under the cycle or condition of Moon, which is peril or undevelopment, lack of competence, restriction.

Now to the favorable side of this figure. What can be done to get any success or satisfaction under this Hexagram? The central line of a Trigram is the intelligent, thinking man. It implies intelligent will under direction and regulation—particularly regulation in this case. The central lines of both Trigrams are Yang—strong—and the lower line of the lower Trigram—physical equipment—is also strong. In summation, let there be the desire for pleasure and satisfaction, *but* let it be confined and regulated by the intellect under will. Only under these conditions can there be the "progress and attainment" as promised in the text. This progress depends solely upon one's intelligent self-regulation. It is also indicated that recourse to one's instincts and intuition help greatly under the conditions of this Hexagram.

In man/woman relationships, it can be either unfavorable or most excellent, depending upon the above conditions.

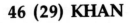

46 (29) KHAN

Moon of Moon

"A perilous defile, or gorge."

In the text we see it is well recognized that a Hexagram is the combination of two Trigrams—one conditioning the other. Here we have both Trigrams the same. The obvious recourse is to name this figure the same as the Trigram. Therefore, the name given by the text.

The advice in the text is to maintain one's own territory and not to advance. Also, that "experience in meeting difficulty makes character." It continues, "It shows the possession of integrity through which the mind is penetrating: do this and it is of high value."

Let us examine this indication of a "penetrating

mind." The central line of a Trigram represents the thinking, intelligent man. In the single Trigram of Moon, the man is in a perilous position because both the upper and lower lines are Yin, which is weakness. The physical body, the lower line, and the higher wisdom or direction, are also weak due to the upper line being a Yin.

But there is one saving grace in this Hexagram. The central line of the upper Trigram (the fifth line) represents the King, or higher intelligence. Thus we have the promise that the exercise and application of the intellect, at its highest, leads one to stand fast amidst the hazardous conditions with a minimum of discomfort or unfavorable influence. Avoid ambitions beyond one's assured abilities.

In man/woman relationships, this must be under intelligent will and direction, without emotions and strong desires.

47 (3) CHUN

Fire of Moon

This is pictorial in the text. It describes the first stage of growth in a plant. From its seed it struggles to arise from out of the earth. This implies initial energy and movement amidst hazards and difficulties.

The lower Trigram is Fire—sudden, exciting energy and action; but it is unfavorable or difficult because of Moon, the upper Trigram. At its best, this is the will breaking up restriction, if under the correct conditions. Because of the daring and impetuous Fire, any movement in advancing should not be lightly undertaken, but only after due and intelligent consideration. There should be correctness, prudence, and effort. It should be well noted that there is no static security indicated. Therefore, no great things should be attempted. Under these conditions, the text predicts "great progress and success." It also states, "The King appoints feudal princes," meaning that the superior person may count on support or help from trusted people of high ability. It also means one may well call to one's aid one's own higher powers, propensities, better instincts, and intuition.

Man/woman relationships: The lower Trigram always represents the woman, and it being Fire, there is exciting energy. This suggests the aggressive type of woman. It is not always favorable.

48 (8) PI

Yoni of Moon

"Union."

The text's implication is that line five, the superior person, may secure the compliance, help, and harmony of all other classes of people. This is the best that can be done, but it is not actually the meaning of the figure.

The lower Trigram is infinite desire and expansion before the difficult, restricted universe. We therefore have a contradiction: Expansion and development versus restriction and difficulty. This is the very unfavorable side of this Hexagram.

Now to the favorable side. The lower Trigram, Yoni, yearns to be filled up—to nourish, support, and develop that which has been initiated by the Yang principle. There is only one Yang line and it is the central line of the superior Trigram, which not only indicates the superior person but also indicates willed, intelligent direction. And *this is the requirement* to get anything favorable from this figure.

One must evoke all his or her sincerity, force, and integrity to bring to his/her support all of that which is indicated by the other five Yin lines; and they are willing supporters, if one carries out the requirements. However, follow the advice of the text: "Let the principal party make sure that his virtue be great, unintermittent, and firm; and let this not be done too late, before the way is exhausted." There are difficulties!

In man/woman relationships it is excellent if the man lives up to the requirements.

49 (34) TA KWANG

Lingam of Fire

"Abundance of strength and vigor."

Clearly, the lower Trigram is the great originating strength, and the upper Trigram is just plain willful, exciting activity. Common sense tells us that under these conditions there can be a drive to unregulated or unrestrained and undirected strength and energy. Obviously one is warned about violent action and contention. Strong action should be held in subordination to intelligence and rightness and exerted only in harmony with it.

Ideally, this is the creative force (Lingam) stimulating and informing the material will, Fire.

Let the superior person use the activity and strength

of the inferiors, and let the inferiors look for permission, or acquiescence of the superior, to exercise this strong activity—but always under the direction of down-to-earth common sense and utility.

In man/woman relationships it should be easily seen that the lower Trigram, the female in this case, is completely masculine. It would be under very rare conditions that this could be regarded as favorable or normal. Success, therefore, demands both natural and firm correctness. At best, it promises no great good fortune or consolidated progress.

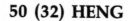

50 (32) HENG

Air of Fire

In the text the subject is "Perseverance in well-doing or in continuously acting out the law of one's being." Actually, one can hardly see anything in this Hexagram that indicates "long continuance."

This "perseverance in well-doing" is merely an ideal, because of the simple fact that the figure almost indicates the contrary! This is one of the 16 Hexagrams where the corresponding lines of each Trigram are of mutual opposite polarity. Therefore, there is a strong rapport between the superior and the inferior that does not promise "long continuance." On the other hand, it indicates easy penetration (Air) by or into sudden, exciting energy, Fire.

This is Air, the mind, informing and assisting the

Fire, or Will. It is the mental concept of physical strength and energy. On the physical plane, the upper Trigram is strong and active; the lower is passive. Thus, movement and easy penetration in any direction is advantageous.

> Lust of result mars will in every way;
> But steadfast purpose spans the vast abyss.
> Maintain thy virtue—heed not criticism;
> Seek not reward—let thy work be its own chrism.
> Passive love wins, where active loses fray,
> And violent efforts end in swift decay.
>
> The G∴B∴G∴ interpretation.

This is the mind assisting one's energetic will, and one should not impetuously change methods.

In man/woman relationships it is favorable for some conditions, according to the foregoing, which also indicates that which is unfavorable.

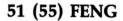

51 (55) FENG

Sun of Fire

"Large and abundant. Prosperity."

This is Sun, the full realization of Fire—energetic will. It is best to receive, maintain, and manifest the realization of the "large and abundant" (brilliant) rather than to be overconcerned with accumulating more, or wanting further advancement. Maintain the development, rather than being concerned with forward movement. There is no need for change. Let one be as the Sun at noon. The superior should employ the talents of the inferiors. The lower Trigram has much of the superiority.

First meet thy mate, then multiply thy force
Be humbly loyal in obscurity;
Let not its accidents disturb thy course.
United with sincerity, 'tis fortune's source.
Then call the clansmen of ability!
Remember: pride and insolence slay majesty.

From the G∴B∴G∴ interpretation

Strangely, although the inferior position is occupied by a Trigram (Sun) that is far superior to the upper Trigram, there is no conflict between them. This figure means inherent brilliance of the exciting, energetic, forceful will. Naturally, if the will is wrong or selfish, this augury can be awkward.

There is certainly no indication of high intelligence in the upper Trigram. We may count on the lower Trigram for the application of intelligent, down-to-earth common sense and practicality toward this energetic drive.

In man/woman relationships it is good for sex magick.

52 (62) HSIAO KWO

Earth of Fire

This Hexagram indicates a restriction of "excessive" activity, but this hardly describes the essential nature and value of this Hexagram.

Philosophically—and perhaps psychologically—the upper Trigram is the subtle behind-the-scenes director. Jung calls it the Daemon. The upper Trigram is the brooding rulership of the eight sub-Trigrams. In this case it is Fire.

Number seven, Fire, exciting energy—a blind drive toward activity. This Trigram has passed through the manifestation of three sub-Trigrams: Lingam, Air, and Sun. It has now reached number four, Earth, which is symbolized as a mountain: stable, fixed, and not movable. Therefore, this is the energy and activity of Fire partly restricted by the fixation of Earth. Here is the great value and condition that the text fails to note. It indicates the conditions where it is both favorable and advisable to fix and consolidate one's affairs rather than to continue an active drive to advance. This is the great value of the figure, and the text rightfully states that aggressive activity can only promise "exceeding in small things." One should even beware of great things or great advancement.

For those who seek the magickal implications, this is the ideal Hexagram for forming and establishing the Magickal Link, or the fixation in matter of the will.

For man/woman relationships, see "consolidation" and "Magickal Link" in the foregoing. It is a time for practical and stable preparation, rather than for active advancement—in any magick.

53 (54) KWEI MEI

Water of Fire

The text intimates, "the youngest daughter improperly initiating her marriage. Under these conditions, action will be evil and in no wise advantageous."

The foregoing describes "a disparity of conditions or things." This disparity is seen to be between Water—pleased satisfaction—and Fire—compelling, energetic action. Certainly, the bad side of this Hexagram indicates the foregoing. Taking stirring, energetic action without due thought to "correctness," in order to attain pleased satisfaction, can ultimately result in dissatisfaction and difficulty.

If the desires are not inordinate, an energetic drive for pleased satisfaction could be of value. Under some circumstances, exciting energy might even be necessary for good results. However, note well, there is an "if" that requires some intelligent restraint and correctness, which might not be duly exercised.

Here is a condition where superiors cannot stir inferiors out of pleased satisfaction. Nor can inferiors reconcile to the stirring energy and activity of the superior. But what is so wrong about an energetic drive to attain pleased satisfaction, if the desires are not excessively inordinate?

In man/woman relationships it is most favorable.

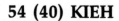

54 (40) KIEH

Moon of Fire

The text name is "Untying a knot or unraveling a complication." No! King Wan got himself in a "knot" in trying to fit this Hexagram in with his ideals of a better state of the kingdom, which was yet to come.

Actually, this Hexagram is of much worse augury than the preceding one.

Number six, Moon, in itself spells more ambition than ability. And when coupled with the stirring energy of Fire, the condition is aggravated. Instead of "untying any knots and untangling obstructions and complications," the exciting energy of Fire makes things worse than ever.

Neither Moon nor Fire is conducive to binding oneself to intelligent regulations. Yet this is the only practical method of avoiding the peril of Moon unless one be greatly superior. The superior person may find circumstances where sudden, quick, energetic action conquers or circumvents the obstruction, restriction, or danger, but he or she must be certain of his/her course.

The text states: "If some operations be called for, there will be good fortune in the early conducting of them." "Early"?—almost immediately!

Considering the nature of this Hexagram, it may even be difficult to make up one's mind not to try any advancement whatsoever, and to be content in amusing oneself in unraveling knots.

In man/woman relationships it is not good. In all matters it is advisable to restrict action as much as possible.

55 (51) KAN

Fire of Fire

"Sudden, moving, exciting energy."

This being the doubled Trigram of Fire, the only recourse for the text is to name it the same as the Trigram.

The G∴B∴G∴ interpretation reads:

Take lofty ground; the tide will ebb and flow
Distraught? May danger teach thee low to go.
Fight fire with fire or sink in mud supine.
Troubles mean profits for men who know.
Caution! Foresee the action of the foe.
Fire! Beware, but smile with mein divine!
Let nothing scare thee: spill no wine!

In the foregoing poetry are the various courses that one may try to take to meet this exciting energy-drive. One should be apprehensive about this moving power and energy. He or she should also cultivate his/her virtue and examine his/her faults. But the big question remains: Just how successfully can one do all of this while being beset with the drive for energetic action?

Let us examine the Hexagram for the best course. The bottom line of both Trigrams is Yang, which is the strength of the physical body and also the strength of the multitudes. Let this be used as an aid. The lines of intelligence and wisdom are Yin, which is a good augury for invoking inspiration. This is the best I can see in this Hexagram.

In man/woman relationships it is not good.

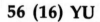

56 (16) YU

Yoni of Fire

"Harmony and contentment."

It is a fact that the ruler of the upper Trigram, Fire, can get the willing and harmonious support of the subject of the lower Trigram, which is Yoni. But King Wan's son seems to have his Trigrams mixed. He writes much about "pleased satisfaction," but this belongs to a different Trigram—the Trigram of Water.

The ruler of the upper Trigram can put all his physical force and energy into action in order to evoke the sustaining and supporting subjects of Yoni, the lower Trigram. Thus, there is harmony between the upper and the lower Trigrams, or the higher forces and the material forces.

The Yang line of the upper Trigram symbolizes the "feudal princes," and King Wan rightfully states: "He may set up and appoint feudal princes to put the hosts in cooperative motion, to advantage."

In summation, it is implied that Yoni gives full nourishment, cooperation, support, and development to the energetic action of Fire. There is great capacity for the awakening force and energy. We should also note the capaciousness of Yoni, which is expansion.

The G∴B∴G∴ interpretation says:

Harmony spreads through all thy coasts.
Appoint thy princes and send forth thine hosts.

In man/woman relationships it is excellent—even for magick.

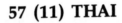

57 (11) THAI

Lingam of Yoni

"Small things gone and great things come."

Here is the great initiating Will combined with the great nourishing and sustaining quality of the upper Trigram of Yoni.

This figure suggests that Heaven is submissive to Earth, which in this particular instance is allowed the dominant force and energy. Yang is always stronger, regardless of its being the upper or lower Trigram of the whole figure.

However, in man/woman relationships, the upper Trigram would be submissive—the man would be submissive to the lower Trigram, which is that of an aggressive woman. See Hexagram number eight for the opposite.

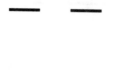

58 (46) SHENG

Air of Yoni

"Advancing upward (in status or attainment).
Ascend the stairs and meet the Great One.
Great progress and success."

The easy penetration of Air combined with the acquiescent support of Yoni assures progress (see the preceding number 57 for more on Yoni being the upper Trigram).

The G∴B∴G∴ interpretation says:

Make thyself welcome with the great; aim high!
Small gifts are sweetened by sincere goodwill.
But empty voids, art thou bold to fill?
The Superior rewards thy true sincerity;

182

Ascend the stairs with proper dignity.
Firm right maintain, though dark the silent sky!

This is the mental image, Air, of Yoni, the infinite desire, or mental concept of the universe. The superior person pays careful attention to his or her virtue and accumulates small developments until it is high and great.

The rulership of the upper Trigram—the central line—indicates a welcoming of the advance of the lower Trigram. There are favorable opportunities with which to advance. Everything in a high position welcomes, sustains, and develops the projection and aspiration of the lower Trigram.

The very ease of advancement of the lower contains the seed of a warning: It is definitely not well to have and to maintain an inordinate desire for more and more advancement. One must realize when, and how, enough is enough.

In man/woman relationships it is not usually good.

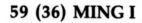

59 (36) MING I

Sun of Yoni

"Intelligence wounded or repressed."

The text advises that it is "advantageous to realize the difficulty of the position." Viewed from the concept of the upper Trigram, which represents a superior person, symbolized as King, the text well names this Hexagram. The upper Trigram consists of three Yin lines from which there is no projective force—it is only weak or receptive.

However, there is another important facet of this: The upper Trigram represents one's own personal spiritual director—the Daemon—one's guiding Genius. In this case, the director is not directing. The upper Trigram, being all Yin, indicates a hands-off attitude of the Director. It gives free consent to the full course of the subject of the lower Trigram, the intelligent person of Earth. In the exercise of his or her intelligence and the expressing of his/her brilliance, he/she has no free reign. However, he or she gets no support from his/her Higher Self, nor any inspiration. Therefore, the scope of his/her achievements is limited.

The text well states that it is advantageous to realize the limitations of the position. This means that it is not well to be overambitious, trying to achieve great things. It is more consistent to be content with a modicum of success. Good luck cannot be relied upon.

In man/woman relationships, it is not good.

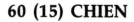

60 (15) CHIEN

Earth of Yoni

"Humility but requiring honor."

Occultly, this is the fixation or restriction in matter of infinite desire. This is materialism carried to a point of fixation. Only with extreme effort or ingenuity can there be any appreciable mobility. Thus, it is said that excesses are diminished and restrictive fixation is increased.

The only Yang line is the upper line of the lower Trigram. This indicates that one should resort to the forces evoked from the religious attitude of humility. The subject is full of desires and he or she may as well reconcile him/herself to self-discipline, for the desires will not avail to him/her very satisfactorily. Aspiration may well be active but accomplishments are not much—for the time being.

The text states that "the Great Stream may be crossed," but this does not apply in a materialistic sense. Rather, it applies to aspiration.

This is the Hexagram of the fertility of Mother Earth. As yet there is no life-giving force of the Sun to initiate it into development.

In man/woman relationships it is not very favorable, unless it be in preparing for consolidation.

61 (19) LIN

Water of Yoni

The text names this "The approach of real authority, or to inspect, comfort, or rule." On the other hand,
King Wan's son treats the six lines under the symbolism of "Advancing." Both are contrived fancy.

The upper Trigram, Yoni, is nourishment and
development of Water, pleased satisfaction. Water
symbolizes a mirror-like reflection, and here we have
a reflection of the formulation of desire—a picture of
the principle of desire—inasmuch as the upper Trigram welcomes or agrees with the expansion of pleased
satisfaction. Higher authority submits to a state of
contentment.

The two lower lines of the lower Trigram being
Yang indicates that the better desires, under the direc-

tion of the intellect, will bring progress and success to attaining a state of pleased satisfaction. This success in material affairs is not on a grand scale, but it is sufficient to give pleased satisfaction and contentment. The bad side of this is desire run rampant.

In man/woman relationships it is satisfactory if confined to the above conditions. It is good for the process known as "Formulation of the Magickal Link," which, under proper direction, brings realization at a later time of development.

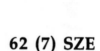

62 (7) SZE

Moon of Yoni

The text intimates the meaning of "The Hosts, or Multitudes." The text often treats the Hexagram from the viewpoint of a military campaign or battle. There is only one Yang line that, by its position, would be a general close to his hosts, or soldiers. The following verse from the G∴B∴G∴ interpretation may provide some sense from the contrived ramblings of King Wan's son:

> Mark well the rules of martial strategy.
> To a chief of the host, the king confers the post.
> Divided counsel—inefficiency!
> Retreat is not an error if need be.
> Seek and destroy bad faith and mutiny!
> But find good men for posts of dignity.

Despite all of the advice of what one should do, the augury of this Hexagram is very unfavorable. In any event, the superior person should not attempt to handle things by him/herself. He or she should, rather, appoint a competent inferior, one of age and experience, to handle his/her problem.

Note that this is the infinite expansion of restriction and inability. The only good promise is that one may entrust the aid of practical and capable people rather than trying to direct the project by him/herself.

In man/woman relationships, there is nothing much to recommend.

63 (24) FU

Fire of Yoni

"Returning. Coming back. Over again."

If we accept the idea that King Wan was a true initiate in the Yi, then we are forced to assume that his very illogical, constricted sequence of the Hexagrams was a secret code to his disciples. If this is the case, we can see how he was caught in his own trap, as exemplified in this Hexagram. This figure is most certainly not the Hexagram of "returning and coming back" from a state of winter, as King Wan describes it. On the contrary, the Trigram of Fire, with the bottom line being Yang—and there are no other Yangs—indicates the first stirring energy and force that initiates winter. But all these interpretations that are based on the seasons are merely digressions.

This Hexagram is strong, exciting action with the energy, Fire, having full free course with Yoni. There is no deterring obstacle except that which is within itself— which is a blind, undirected or misdirected, active energy.

There is no guarantee that this energetic drive for activity will be intelligently directed, but if it is, there will be advantage in the movement. Misdirected energy and sudden drives remain a constant warning. This is an augury that can be good for starting things if they are handled correctly and intelligently, but it is not for finishing things.

64 (2) KHWAN

Yoni of Yoni

Since this is Khwan doubled, the implications of this figure are simply an intensification of the Trigram.

There is great receptivity, nourishment, development, and great capacity of wide comprehension, but all this is mere potential until the action of Yang unites with Yin. There is not a single Yang line in this Hexagram. The egg, or Yin, is nothing without the fertilization or union with Yang. The fertility and development of Earth is nothing without the stimulating action or impregnation of the Yang.

What then can we expect from this Hexagram? Any project must rest in the Great Womb of Time until a Yang force stimulates it into action.

If there is any promise at all in this Hexagram, it is

that it rests safely in the womb, awaiting the initiatory force to stimulate its development. However, one may also receive, but the text correctly states that "if he takes the initiative in any movement, he will go astray." On the other hand, "If he follow, he will find his proper direction."

This Hexagram indicates a propitious time to receive and to collect resources and sustaining power for future action.

Appendix

*Hints on Making Your Own Interpretations
of the Hexagrams.*

In considering the thousand and one different questions that may be posed to the Yi, it is obvious that no text can give specific answers to any of these questions. Therefore some rules of analysis must be given as guides. Throughout the foregoing descriptions of the 64 Hexagrams, many of these rules have been stated by showing the reasoning that directs the determination; however, the serious student will find additional guidelines here given pertaining to the significance of each line position (whether Yang or Yin), and secondly, whether the corresponding line positions of the two component Trigrams are in mutual cooperation (i.e., opposite polarity—one Yang and one Yin).

Once again, refer to the table of correspondences (page 58) of the combined Trigrams. It is well to keep in mind also the keywords of the three line positions of the single Trigram, as follows:

Line 1: Man of EARTH (Troglodyte)
Line 2: MIND of Man (Thinking Man)
Line 3: HEAVEN-inspired Man (Man of True Genius)

The next step is to examine the import of the various line positions as to whether Yang or Yin. In this, we begin with those Hexagrams that have a *singleton* (i.e, one line position which is one polarity and all the other five positions are of opposite polarity).

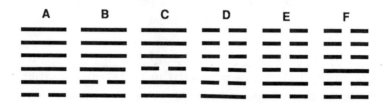

When these Trigrams are reversed (the lower Trigram placed in the upper position), it makes six more Hexagrams. The total is six plus six—twelve hexes in which there is a singleton—no small number. Now to the significance of a singleton.

It is now over 40 years ago that Marc Edmund Jones called attention to the significance of the singleton in astrology, i.e., when there is only one planet in one of the hemispheres and all of the other planets are in the opposite hemisphere. The correct analysis of this phenomenon is that special emphasis is thrown upon the singleton, *always*, in reading the chart, ranging from those *fixations* of a psychopathic personality on up to the special fixation in which real genius is expressed. Now then, the singleton in the Yi is to be regarded in the same way.

If the singleton is a Yin, then the judgment is not to be confined to the polarity response of the corresponding Yang line in the other Trigram. No! That Yin line supplements the activity of all of the five Yang lines. It may be also said to be a sort of fixation.

Let us be thoroughly prepared to analyze the 12 singleton Hexagrams. In this, we should discuss the three key foundation stones of the Yi: the Great Triad—ACTIVITY, SUBSTANCE and FORM, which operates in both the animate and inanimate world. Let us begin with a simple illustration—almost too simple, in fact. A man directs his "activity" upon a certain facet of "substance" (wood, for example) and the impression of the activity upon the substance produces a manifested "form" of a chair or table.

Marc Edmund Jones has treated this concept extensively in his astrological work. The planets are the initiating activity; the signs of the zodiac are the different kinds of facets of substance; and the various houses show where the union of activity and substance produces the final manifested form. The Yi Basic is the same: The Yang is the initiating activity, and the specialization of this activity is based upon the nature of the occupied line positions. The responding Yin is the substance. The union of Yang (activity) with Yin (substance) produces the resultant manifested form, the nature of the manifested form being determined mostly by the nature of the line position held by Yin. The reason for this is that Yin is the nourisher and developer of form manifestation, much more so than Yang, which is only the initiating force. It is for this same reason that the lower Trigram is the Trigram of material, physical manifestation—form. The lower Trigram is the Yin Trigram, essentially, while the upper Trigram is essentially the Yang Trigram.

We are now prepared to analyze the several singleton Hexagrams.

Hexagram A (#2): The bottom line (Yin) is the desires and instincts of the self-seeking kind, be it conscious or unconscious. The Yin womb yearns to be "filled up" with the Yang initiating force to nourish and develop the offspring manifestation—whether the woman be conscious of it or not. King Wan described the Hexagram very well in giving the symbol of a "bold woman" who supports (or even supplants) the great Yang force of the other five lines. But "do not wed her, nor associate with her long," he cautions, for then Yang would be wasting his force. This is a good metaphor and applies in all ways. As a project it applies to a peanut stand rather than to a big project such as building a bridge. (Refer back to chapter 5 for more on this Hexagram.)

Hexagram B (#3): The singleton is in the central line of the lower Hexagram. This line is man as a thinker. It being Yin means that men are invoking good thinking and intelligence. Hence the Hexagram is well named as Union of Men. There is little of the feminine element in this Hexagram. (See Hexagram number three in chapter 5.)

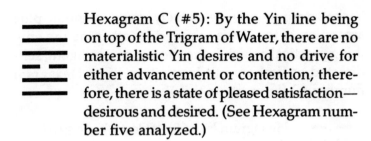

Hexagram C (#5): By the Yin line being on top of the Trigram of Water, there are no materialistic Yin desires and no drive for either advancement or contention; therefore, there is a state of pleased satisfaction—desirous and desired. (See Hexagram number five analyzed.)

Now follows the three Hexagrams where the singleton is Yang instead of Yin. Instead of being passive, yearning, supplementing, and desirous, as with the Yin singleton, the Yang singleton projects active initiating energy and force and can even be combative.

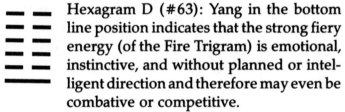

Hexagram D (#63): Yang in the bottom line position indicates that the strong fiery energy (of the Fire Trigram) is emotional, instinctive, and without planned or intelligent direction and therefore may even be combative or competitive.
(See analysis of Hexagram number 63 for more light on the import of this singleton.)

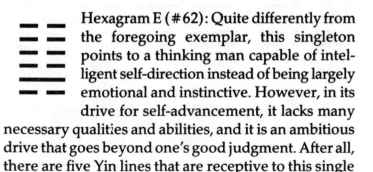

Hexagram E (#62): Quite differently from the foregoing exemplar, this singleton points to a thinking man capable of intelligent self-direction instead of being largely emotional and instinctive. However, in its drive for self-advancement, it lacks many necessary qualities and abilities, and it is an ambitious drive that goes beyond one's good judgment. After all, there are five Yin lines that are receptive to this single

Yang; consequently, selectively directed intent plus aspiration of the Yin is required for attaining the only thing practical, which is the success of intelligent, self-directed aspiration and inspiration. (See Hexagram number 62 for more on this.)

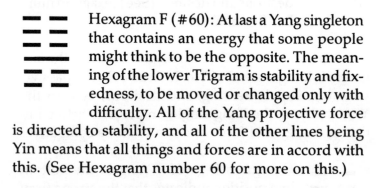 Hexagram F (#60): At last a Yang singleton that contains an energy that some people might think to be the opposite. The meaning of the lower Trigram is stability and fixedness, to be moved or changed only with difficulty. All of the Yang projective force is directed to stability, and all of the other lines being Yin means that all things and forces are in accord with this. (See Hexagram number 60 for more on this.)

Now if the positions of the Trigrams are reversed, we see that the singleton Trigram is the top Trigram instead of the lower.

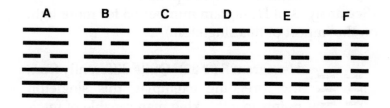

One should now review what has been said about these Hexagrams in the text, particularly in reference to the treatment of the two responding lines. At the same time, one should again refer to what is written herein about the first set of the six singleton Hexagrams in order to see where and how there is considerable difference in meaning when the positions of the Trigrams are reversed.

Now to an example of a Hexagram in which there are two line positions of polarity response.

This Hexagram, number 18, is named the Cauldron because it transforms various substances, by heat, into food that is fit for human consumption. Hence it is the Great Transformer of things and people.

Reasoning: The bottom Yin line of the Air Trigram *receives* the projection of the Yang line of the Sun Trigram. The Sun Trigram means "brilliant realization," therefore it is strong emotions, instincts, and physical equipment that is received by the lower Trigram. In turn, the Air Trigram projects strong thinking and self-directing strength and ability to the central Yin line of the upper Trigram, and take note that this is enhanced by the fact that the projecting line is Air, which in itself means mental ability and good mental concepts. In short, both Trigrams receive from each other those qualities in which they are weak: The two Trigrams mutually strengthen each other. It is not necessary, however, for the student to go into such complex reasoning. It is sufficient to see how the "inferior" can benefit from the bottom Yang line of the "superior" and how the superior can benefit from the lower Yin line of the inferior—and how the questioner can take advantage of these conditions in order to bring the object of the question to a better resolution.

In this example (number 50) we have a Hexagram that is the same, in appearance, with the foregoing example, with the exception that the top line of the upper Trigram is Yin instead of Yang, thus making all three lines of the two Trigrams mutually responsive. But that is not all—we have changed the upper Trigram from Sun to Fire.

It is sufficient that the questioner reason out the following and pursue the objective in accordance with the advised conditions.

First, the easygoing, easily penetrated Air Trigram receives the energy and substantiality from the responding bottom Yang line of the upper Trigram of Fire. The Fire Trigram, which is lacking in intelligent self-direction, benefits from the opposite polarity Yang of the lower Trigram and also receives some of the higher wisdom in its upper Yin Line. It boils down to Air, the mind, assisting and informing the great physical energy of Fire. It is, of course, up to the consultant to figure out what to do and what not to do to bring the subject of the question to its best outcome. One thing is certainly very clear—the "superior" can benefit from the mind and intelligence of the "inferior." (Note: see Hexagram number 50 in chap. 5.)

SEX MAGICK
by Louis T. Culling

In sexual union there is a uniting of magnetic and electric currents to create a field of energy that extends both inward and outward to contact the infinite Intelligence and the personal unconscious. In perfecting this union lies Magick, for we gain insight and extend our personal power by becoming a channel to the powers of the universe.

In *Sex Magick* the long hidden secrets and principles of sex magick are revealed with examples that enable one to turn sexual union into a valid tool for mystical ecstasy and self-transcendence.

This is *not* the magic of sex; Sex Magick is using sex as a potent vehicle for magical attainment. Its purpose is to accomplish the mystical union of normal consciousness with the highest consciousness. It embraces a healthy psychological view of man, allowing him to grow and create without restriction. Sex Magick is unsurpassed for achieving the highest physical and spiritual ecstasies.

0-87542-110-5, 148 pages, 5¼ x 8, softcover   **$6.95**

THE GOLDEN DAWN
by Israel Regardie

The Original Account of the Teachings, Rites and Ceremonies of the Hermetic Order of the Golden Dawn as revealed by Israel Regardie, with further revision, expansion, and additional notes by Israel Regardie, Cris Monnastre, and others.

Originally published in four bulky volumes of some 1200 pages, this 5th Revised and Enlarged Edition has been entirely reset in modern, less space-consuming type, in half the pages (while retaining the original pagination in marginal notation for reference) for greater ease and use.

Corrections of typographical errors perpetuated in the original and subsequent editions have been made, with further revision and additional text and notes by actual practitioners of the Golden Dawn system of Magick, with an Introduction by the only student ever accepted for personal training by Regardie.

Also included are Initiation Ceremonies, important rituals for consecration and invocation, methods of meditation and magical working based on the Enochian Tablets, studies in the Tarot, and the system of Qabalistic Correspondences that unite the World's religions and magical traditions into a comprehensive and practical whole.

This volume is designed as a study and practice curriculum suited to both group and private practice. Meditation upon, and following with the Active Imagination, the Initiation Ceremonies is fully experiential without need of participation in group or lodge.

0-87542-663-8, 744 pages, 6 x 9, illus.   **$19.95**

THE KWAN YIN BOOK OF CHANGES
Diane Stein

The Kwan Yin Book of Changes places the ancient Chinese *I Ching*, a divinatory system much a complement to the tarot, in a context that women and men in touch with peace can relate to. The patriarchalism and rigidity of the traditional *I Ching* is exchanged for a women-only communal government and world, with situations and language relevant to modern occult women and to men who relate to the feminine aspects of themselves. The God/Emperor of traditional translations is replaced by the immanence of the Earth and the Goddess, and fate and predistiny give way to free will and choice. The Superior Man of the old versions is the Superior or Spiritual Woman in a system much more positive than any earlier *I Ching* translation.

As a divinatory took, *The Kwan Yin Book of Changes* returns the Chinese *I Ching* to women's use, and is a tool of great power simple to use. The book stands the *I Ching* side by side with the tarot as an aspect of women's spirituality, and is a remembering of the submerged skills of women's matriarchy and culture.

0-87542-760-X, 256 pages, 6 x 9, illus., softcover. **$9.95**

AUTHENTIC CHINESE COINS

The I Ching divinatory system becomes even more interesting if you use genuine Chinese coins. These authentic coins were purchased expressly for use with *The Kwan Yin Book of Changes*. These coins were made during the reign of Emperor Chen Lung, dated 1736. They are made of a brass/copper combination. The square hole in the middle allowed the Chinese to carry their money on a string tied around their waist.

These unique coins come in sets of three, and are attractive, with authentic Chinese lettering engraved on them. They are unique divinatory tools, and will make your contact with Kwan Yin easier and more genuine.

COINS **Set of three, $2.00**